ACADIA;

OR,

A MONTH WITH THE BLUE NOSES.

FREDERIC S. COZZENS,

[ZHINGOORA BOOKS]

This edition is published by
Zhingoora Books.

The Cover is Designed by Pallav Sethiya.

PREFACE.

As I have a sort of religion in literature, believing that no author can justly intrude upon the public without feeling that his writings may be of some benefit to mankind, I beg leave to apologize for this little book. I know, no critic can tell me better than I know myself, how much it falls short of what might have been done by an abler pen. Yet it is something—an index, I should say, to something better. The French in America may sometime find a champion. For my own part, I would that the gentler principles which governed them, and the English under William Penn, and the Dutch under the enlightened rule of the States General, had obtained here, instead of the narrower, the more penurious, and most prescriptive policy of their neighbors.

I am indebted to Judge Haliburton's "History of Nova Scotia" for the main body of historical facts in this volume. Let me acknowledge my obligations. His researches and impartiality are most creditable, and worthy of respect and attention. I have also drawn as liberally as time and space would permit from chronicles contemporary with the events of those early days, as well as from a curious collection of items relating to the subject, cut from the London newspapers a hundred years ago, and kindly furnished me by Geo. P. Putnam, Esq. These are always the surest guides. To Mrs. Kate Williams, of Providence, R. I., I am indebted also. Her story of the "Neutral French," no doubt, inspired the author of the most beautiful pastoral in the language. The "Evangeline" of Longfellow, and the "Pauline" of this lady's legend, are pictures of the same individual, only drawn by different hands.

A word in regard to the two Acadian portraits. These are literal ambrotypes, to which Sarony has added a few touches of his artistic crayon. It may interest the reader to know that these are the first, the only likenesses of the real Evangelines of Acadia. The women of Chezzetcook appear at day-break in the city of Halifax, and as soon as the sun is up vanish like the dew. They have usually a basket of fresh eggs, a brace or two of worsted socks, a bottle of fir-balsam to sell. These comprise their simple commerce. When the market-bell rings you find them not. To catch such fleeting phantoms, and to transfer them to the frontispiece of a book published here, is like painting the burnished wings of a humming-bird. A friend, however, undertook the task. He rose before the sun, he bought eggs, worsted socks, and fir-balsam of the Acadians. By constant attentions he became acquainted [Pg v] with a pair of Acadian women, niece and aunt. Then he proposed the matter to them:

"I want you to go with me to the daguerreotype gallery."

"What for?"

"To have your portraits taken."

"What for?"

"To send to a friend in New York."

"What for?"

"To be put in a book."

"What for?"

"Never mind 'what for,' will you go?"

Aunt and niece—both together in a breath—"No."

So my friend, who was a wise man, wrote to the priest of the settlement of Chezzetcook, to explain the "what for," and the consequence was—these portraits! But these women had a terrible time at the head of the first flight of stairs. Not an inch would these shy creatures budge beyond. At last, the wife of the operator induced them to rise to the high flight that led to the Halifax skylight, and there they were painted by the sun, as we see them now.

Nothing more! Ring the bell, prompter, and draw the curtain.

CONTENTS.

CHAPTER I.

CHAPTER II.

CHAPTER III.

CHAPTER IV.

CHAPTER V.

hand at a Fish-pugh

CHAPTER XV.

CHAPTER XVI.

CHAPTER XVII.

CHAPTER XVIII.

ACADIA.

CHAPTER I.

Vague Rumors of Nova Scotia—A Fortnight upon Salt Water—Interesting Sketch of the Atlantic—Halifax!—Determine to stay in the Province—Province Building and Pictures—Coast Scenery—Liberty in Language, and Aspirations of the People—Evangeline and Relics of Acadia—Market-Place—The Encampment at Point Pleasant—Kissing Bridge—The "Himalaya"—A Sabbath in a Garrison Town—Grand Celebration of the Peace, and Natal Day of Halifax—And a Hint of a Visit to Chezzetcook.

It is pleasant to visit Nova Scotia in the month of June. Pack up your flannels and your fishing tackle, leave behind you your prejudices and your summer clothing, take your trout-pole in one hand and a copy of Haliburton in the other, and step on board a Cunarder at Boston. In thirty-six hours you are in the loyal little province, and above you floats the red flag and the cross of St. George. My word for it, you will not regret the trip. That the idea of visiting Nova Scotia ever struck any living person as something peculiarly pleasant and cheerful, is not within the bounds of probability. Very rude people are wont to speak of Halifax in connection with the name of a place never alluded to in polite society—except by clergymen. As for the rest of the Province, there are certain vague rumors of extensive and constant fogs, but nothing more. The land is a sort of terra incognita. Many take it to be a part of Canada, and others firmly believe it is somewhere in Newfoundland.

In justice to Nova Scotia, it is proper to state that the Province is a province by itself; that it hath its own governor and parliament, and its own proper and copper currency. How I chanced to go there was altogether a matter of destiny. It was a severe illness—a gastric disorder of the most obstinate kind, that cast me upon its balmy shores. One day, after a protracted relapse, as I was creeping feebly along Broadway, sunning myself, like a March fly on a window-pane, whom should I meet but St. Leger, my friend. "You look pale," said St. Leger. To which I replied by giving him a full, complete, and accurate history of my ailments, after the manner of valetudinarians. "Why do you not try change of air?" he asked; and then briskly added, "You could spare a couple of weeks or so, could you not, to go to the Springs?" "I could," said I, feebly. "Then," said St. Leger, "take the two weeks' time, but do not go to the Springs. Spend your fortnight on the salt water— get out of sight of land—that is the thing for you." And so, shaking my hand warmly, St. Leger passed on, and left me to my reflections.

A fortnight upon salt water? Whither? Cape Cod at once loomed up; Nantucket, and Martha's Vineyard. "And why not the Bermudas?" said a voice within me; "the enchanted Islands of Prospero, and Ariel, and Miranda; of Shakspeare, and Raleigh, and Irving?" And echo answered: "Why not?"

It is but a day-and-a-half's sail to Halifax; thence, by a steamer, to those neighboring isles; for the Curlew and the Merlin, British mail-boats, leave Halifax fortnightly for the Bermudas. A thousand miles of life-invigorating atmosphere—a week upon salt water, and you are amid the magnificent scenery of the Tempest!

And how often had the vague desire impressed me—how often, indeed, had I visited, in imagination, those beautiful scenes, those islands which have made Shakspeare our near kinsman; which are part and parcel of the romantic history of Sir Walter Raleigh! For, even if he do describe them, in his strong old Saxon, as "the Bermudas, a hellish sea for Thunder, and Lightning, and Storms," yet there is a charm even in this description, for doubtless these very words gave a title to the great drama of William of Stratford, and suggested the idea of

"The still-vexed Bermoöthes."

Ah, yes! and who that has read Irving's "Three Kings of Bermuda" has not felt the influence of those Islas Encantadas—those islands of palms and coral, of orange groves and ambergris! "A fortnight?" said I, quoting St. Leger; "I will take a month for it." And so, in less than a week from the date of his little prescription, I was bidding farewell to some dear friends, from the deck of the "Canada," at East Boston wharf, as Captain Lang, on the top of our wheel-house, shouted out, in a very briny voice: "Let go the starboard bow chain—go slow!"

It would be presumptuous in me to speak of the Atlantic, from the limited acquaintance I had with it. The note-book of an invalid for two days at sea, with a heavy ground swell, and the wind in the most favorable quarter, can scarcely be attractive. As the breeze freshened, and the tars of old England ran aloft, to strip from the black sails the wrappers of white canvas that had hid them when in port; and as these leathern, bat-like pinions spread out on each side of the funnel, there was a moment's glimpse of the picturesque; but it was a glimpse only, and no more. One does not enjoy the rise and dip of the bow of a steamer, at first, however graceful it may be in the abstract. To be sure, there were some things else interesting. For instance, three brides aboard! And one of them lovely enough to awaken interest, on sea or land, in any body but a Halifax passenger. I hope those fair ladies will have a pleasant tour, one and all, and that the view they take of the great world, so early in life, will make them more contented with that minor world, henceforth to be within the limits of their dominion. Lullaby to the young wives! there will be rocking enough anon!

But we coasted along pleasantly enough the next day, within sight of the bold headlands of Maine; the sky and sea clear of vapor, except the long reek from the steamer's pipe. And then came nightfall and the northern stars; and, later at night, a new luminary on the edge of the horizon—Sambro' light; and then a sudden quenching of stars, and horizon, lighthouse, ropes, spars, and smoke stack; the sounds of hoarse voices of command in the obscurity; a trampling of men; and then down went the anchor in the ooze, and the Canada was fog-bound in the old harbor of Chebucto for the night, within a few miles of the city.

But with the early dawn, we awoke to hear the welcome sounds of the engines in motion, and when we reached the deck, the mist was drifted with sunlight, and rose and fell in luminous billows on water and shore, and then lifted, lingered, and vanished!

"And this is Halifax?" said I, as that quaint, mouldy old town poked its wooden gables through the fog of the second morning. "This is Halifax? This the capital of Nova Scotia? This the city that harbored those loyal heroes of the Revolution, who gallantly and gayly fought, and bled, and ran for their king? Ah! you brave old Tories; you staunch upholders of the crown; cavaliers without ringlets or feathers, russet boots or steeple-crown hats, it seems as if you were still hovering over this venerable tabernacle of seven hundred gables, and wreathing each particular ridge-pole, pigeon-hole, and shingle with a halo of fog."

The plank was laid, and the passengers left the steamer. There were a few vehicles on the wharf for the accommodation of strangers; square, black, funereal-like, wheeled sarcophagi, eminently suggestive of burials and crape. Of course I did not ride in one, on account of unpleasant associations; but, placing my trunk in charge of a cart-boy with a long-tailed dray, and a diminutive pony, I walked through the silent streets towards "The Waverley."

It was an inspiriting morning, that which I met upon the well-docked shores of Halifax, and although the side-walks of the city were neither bricked nor paved with flags, and the middle street was in its original and aboriginal clay, yet there was novelty in making its acquaintance. Everybody was asleep in that early fog; and when everybody woke up, it was done so quietly that the change was scarcely apparent.

But the "Merlin," British mailer, is to sail at noon for the Shakspeare Island, and breakfast must be discussed, and then once more I am with you, my anti-bilious ocean. It chanced, however, I heard at breakfast, that the "Curlew," the mate of the "Merlin," had been lost a short time before at sea, and as there was but one, and not two steamers on the route, so that I would be detained longer with Prospero and Miranda than might be comfortable in the approaching hot weather, it came to pass that I had reluctantly to forego the projected voyage, and anchor my trunk of tropical clothing in room Number Twenty, Hotel Waverley. It was a great disappointment, to be sure, after such brilliant anticipations—but what is life without philosophy? When we cannot get what we wish, let us take what we may. Let the "Merlin" sail! I will visit, instead of those Islas Encantadas, "The Acadian land on the shore of the Basin of Minas." Let the "Merlin" sail! I will see the ruined walls of Louisburgh, and the harbors that once sheltered the Venetian sailor, Cabot. "Let her sail!" said I, and when the morn passed I saw her slender thread of smoke far off on the glassy ocean, without a sigh of regret, and resolutely turned my face from the promised palms to welcome the sturdy pines of the province.

The city hill of Halifax rises proudly from its wharves and shipping in a multitude of mouse-colored wooden houses, until it is crowned by the citadel. As it is a garrison town, as well as a naval station, you meet in the streets red-coats and blue-jackets without number; yonder, with a brilliant staff, rides the Governor, Sir John Gaspard le Marchant, and here, in a carriage, is Admiral Fanshawe, C.B., of the "Boscawen" Flag-ship. Every thing is suggestive of impending hostilities; war, in burnished trappings, encounters you at the street corners, and the air vibrates from time to time with bugles, fifes, and drums. But oh! what a slow place it is! Even two Crimean regiments with medals and decorations could not wake it up. The little old houses seem to look with wondrous apathy as these pass by, as though they had given each other a quiet nudge with their quaint old gables, and whispered: "Keep still!"

I wandered up and down those old streets in search of something picturesque, but in vain; there was scarcely any thing remarkable to arrest or interest a stranger. Such, too, might have been the appearance of other places I wot of, if those staunch old loyalists had had their way in the days gone by!

But the Province House, which is built of a sort of yellow sandstone, with pillars in front, and trees around it, is a well-proportioned building, with an air of great solidity and respectability. There are in it very fine full-lengths of King George II. and Queen Caroline, and two full-lengths of King George III. and Queen Charlotte; a full-length of Chief-Justice Haliburton, and another full-length, by Benjamin West, of another chief-justice, in a red robe and a formidable wig. Of these portraits, the two first-named are the most attractive; there is something so gay and festive in the appearance of King George II. and Queen Caroline, so courtly and sprightly, so graceful and amiable, that one is tempted to exclaim: "Bless the painter! what a genius he had!"

And now, after taking a look at Dalhousie College with the parade in front, and the square town-clock, built by his graceless Highness the Duke of Kent, let us climb Citadel Hill, and see the formidable protector of town and harbor. Lively enough it is, this great stone fortress, with its soldiers, swarming in and out like bees, and the glimpses of country and harbor are surpassingly beautiful; but just at the margin of this slope below us, is the street, and that dark fringe of tenements skirting the edge of this green glacis is, I fear me, filled with vicious inmates. Yonder, where the blackened ruins of three houses are visible, a sailor was killed and thrown out of a window not long since, and his shipmates burned the houses down in consequence; there is something strikingly suggestive in looking upon this picture and on that.

But if you cast your eyes over yonder magnificent bay, where vessels bearing flags of all nations are at anchor, and then let your vision sweep past and over the islands to the outlets beyond, where the quiet ocean lies, bordered with fog-banks that loom ominously at the boundary-line of the horizon, you will see a picture of marvellous beauty; for the coast scenery here transcends our own sea-shores, both in color and outline. And behind us again stretch large green plains, dotted with cottages, and bounded with undulating hills, with now and then glimpses of blue water; and as we walk down Citadel Hill, we feel half-reconciled to Halifax, its queer little streets, its quaint, mouldy old gables, its soldiers and sailors, its fogs, cabs, penny and half-penny tokens, and all its little, odd, outlandish peculiarities. Peace be with it! after all, it has a quiet charm for an invalid!

The inhabitants of Halifax exhibit no trifling degree of freedom in language for a loyal people; they call themselves "Halligonians." This title, however, is sometimes pronounced "'Alligonians," by the more rigid, as a mark of respect to the old country. But innovation has been at work even here, for the majority of Her Majesty's subjects aspirate the letter H. Alas for innovation! who knows to what results this trifling error may lead? When

Mirabeau went to the French court without buckles in his shoes, the barriers of etiquette were broken down, and the Swiss Guards fought in vain.

There is one virtue in humanity peculiarly grateful to an invalid; to him most valuable, by him most appreciated, namely, hospitality. And that the 'Alligonians are a kind and good people, abundant in hospitality, let me attest. One can scarcely visit a city occupied by those whose grandsires would have hung your rebel grandfathers (if they had caught them), without some misgivings. But I found the old Tory blood of three Halifax generations, yet warm and vital, happy to accept again a rebellious kinsman, a real live Yankee, in spite of Sam Slick and the Revolution.

Let us take a stroll through these quiet streets. This is the Province House with its Ionic porch, and within it are the halls of Parliament, and offices of government. You see there is a red-coat with his sentry-box at either corner. Behind the house again are two other sentries on duty, all glittering with polished brass, and belted, gloved, and bayoneted, in splendid style. Of what use are these satellites, except to watch the building and keep it from running away? On the street behind the Province House is Fuller's American Book-store, which we will step into, and now among these books, fresh from the teeming presses of the States, we feel once more at home. Fuller preserves his equanimity in spite of the blandishments of royalty, and once a year, on the Fourth of July, hoists the "stars and stripes," and bravely takes dinner with the United States Consul, in the midst of lions and unicorns. Many pleasant hours I passed with Fuller, both in town and country.

Near by, on the next corner, is the print-store of our old friends the Wetmores, and here one can see costly engravings of Landseer's fine pictures, and indeed whole portfolios of English art. But of all the pictures there was one, the most touching, the most suggestive! The presiding genius of the place, the unsceptred Queen of this little realm was before me—Faed's Evangeline! And this reminded me that I was in the Acadian land! This reminded me of Longfellow's beautiful pastoral, a poem that has spread a glory over Nova Scotia, a romantic interest, which our own land has not yet inspired! I knew that I was in Acadia; the historic scroll unrolled and stretched its long perspective to earlier days; it recalled De Monts, and the la Tours; Vice Admiral Destournelle, who ran upon his own sword, hard by, at Bedford Basin; and the brave Baron Castine.

The largest settlement of the Acadians is in the neighborhood of Halifax. In the early mornings, you sometimes see a few of these people in the streets, or at the market, selling a dozen or so of fresh eggs, or a pair or two of woollen socks, almost the only articles of their simple commerce. But you must needs be early to see them; after eight o'clock, they will have all vanished. Chezzetcook, or, as it is pronounced by the 'Alligonians, "Chizzencook," is twenty-two miles from Halifax, and as the Acadian peasant has neither horse nor mule, he or she must be off betimes to reach home before mid-day nuncheon. A score of miles on foot is no trifle, in all weathers, but Gabriel and Evangeline perform it cheerfully; and when the knitting-needle and the poultry shall have replenished their slender stock, off again they will start on their midnight pilgrimage, that they may reach the great city of Halifax before day-break.

We must see Chezzetcook anon, gentle reader.

Let us visit the market-place. Here is Masaniello, with his fish in great profusion. Codfish, three-pence or four-pence each; lobsters, a penny; and salmon of immense size at six-pence a pound (currency), equal to a dime of our money. If you prefer trout, you must buy them of these Micmac squaws in traditional blankets, a shilling a bunch; and you may also buy baskets of rainbow tints from these copper ladies for a mere trifle; and as every race has a separate vocation here, only of the negroes can you purchase berries. "This is a busy town," one would say, drawing his conclusion from the market-place; for the shifting crowd, in all costumes and in all colors, Indians, negroes, soldiers, sailors, civilians, and Chizzincookers, make up a pageant of no little theatrical effect and bustle. Again: if you are still strong in limb, and ready for a longer walk, which I, leaning upon my staff, am not, we will visit the encampment at Point Pleasant. The Seventy-sixth Regiment has pitched its tents here among the evergreens. Yonder you see the soldiers, looking like masses of red fruit amidst the spicy verdure of the spruces. Row upon row of tents, and file upon file of men standing at ease, each one before his knapsack, his little leather household, with its shoes, socks, shirts, brushes, razors, and other furniture open for inspection. And there is Sir John Gaspard le Marchant, with a brilliant staff, engaged in the pleasant duty of picking a personal quarrel with each medal-decorated hero, and marking down every hole in his socks, and every gap in his comb, for the honor of the service. And this

Point Pleasant is a lovely place, too, with a broad look-out in front, for yonder lies the blue harbor and the ocean deeps. Just back of the tents is the cookery of the camp, huge mounds of loose stones, with grooves at the top, very like the architecture of a cranberry-pie; and if the simile be an homely one, it is the best that comes to mind to convey an idea of those regimental stoves, with their seams and channels of fire, over which potatoes bubble, and roast and boiled scud forth a savory odor. And here and there, wistfully regarding this active scene, amid the green shrubbery, stands a sentinel before his sentry-box, built of spruce boughs, wrought into a mimic military temple, and fanciful enough, too, for a garden of roses. And look you now! If here be not Die Vernon, with "habit, hat, and feather," cantering gayly down the road between the tents, and behind her a stately groom in gold-lace band, top-boots, and buck-skins. A word in your ear—that pleasant half-English face is the face of the Governor's daughter.

The road to Point Pleasant is a favorite promenade in the long Acadian twilights. Mid-way between the city and the Point lies "Kissing Bridge," which the Halifax maidens sometimes pass over. Who gathers toll nobody knows, but I thought there was a mischievous glance in the blue eyes of those passing damsels that said plainly they could tell, "an' they would." I love to look upon those happy, healthy English faces; those ruddy cheeks, flushed with exercise, and those well-developed forms, not less attractive because of the sober-colored dresses and brown flat hats, in which, o' summer evenings, they glide towards the mysterious precincts of "The Bridge." What a tale those old arches could tell? ¿Quien sabe? Who knows?

But next to "Kissing Bridge," the prominent object of interest, now, to Halifax ladies, is the great steamer that lies at the Admiralty, the Oriental screw-steamer Himalaya—the transport ship of two regiments of the heroes of Balaklava, and Alma, and Inkerman, and Sebastopol. A vast specimen of naval architecture; an unusual sight in these waters; a marine vehicle to carry twenty-five hundred men! Think of this moving town; this portable village of royal belligerents covered with glory and medals, breasting the billows! Is there not something glorious in such a spectacle? And yet I was told by a brave officer, who wore the decorations of the four great battles on his breast, that of his regiment, the Sixty-third, but thirty men were now living, and of the thirty, seventeen only were able to attend drill. That regiment numbered a thousand at Alma!

No gun broke the silence of the Sabbath morning, as the giant ship moved from the Admiralty, on the day following our visit to Point Pleasant, and silently furrowed her path oceanward on her return to Gibraltar. A long line of thick bituminous smoke, above the low house-tops, was the only hint of her departure, to the citizens. It was a grand sight to see her vast bulk moving among the islands in the harbor, almost as large as they.

And now, being Sunday, after looking in at the Cathedral, which does not represent the usual pomp of the Romish Church, we will visit the Garrison Chapel. A bugle-call from barracks, or Citadel Hill, salutes us as we stroll towards the chapel; otherwise, Halifax is quiet, as becomes the day. Presently we see the long scarlet lines approaching, and presently the men, with orderly step, file from the street through the porch into the gallery and pews. Then the officers of field and line, of ordnance and commissary departments, take their allotted seats below. Then the chimes cease, and the service begins. Most devoutly we prayed for the Queen, and omitted the President of the United States.

As the Crimeans ebbed from the church, and, floating off in the distance, wound slowly up Citadel Hill against the quiet clear summer sky, I could not but think of these lines from Thomas Miller's "Summer Morning:"

"A troop of soldiers pass with stately pace, Their early music wakes the village street: Through yon turned blinds peeps many a lovely face, Smiling perchance unconsciously how sweet! One does the carpet press with blue-veined feet, Not thinking how her fair neck she exposes, But with white foot timing the drum's deep beat; And when again she on her pillow dozes, Dreams how she'll dance that tune 'mong summer's sweetest roses

"So let her dream, even as beauty should! Let the while plumes athwart her slumbers away! Why should I steep their swaling snows in blood, Or bid her think of battle's grim array? Truth will too soon her blinding star display, And like a fearful comet meet her eyes. And yet how peaceful they pass on their way! How grand the sight as up the hill they rise! *I will not think of cities reddening in the skies.*"

It was my fate to see next day a great celebration. It was the celebration of peace between England and Russia. Peace having been proclaimed, all Halifax was in arms! Loyalty threw out her bunting to the breeze, and fired her crackers. The civic authorities presented an address to the royal representative of Her Majesty, requesting His Excellency to transmit the same to the foot of the throne. Militia-men shot off municipal cannon; bells echoed from the belfries; the shipping fluttered with signals; and Citadel Hill telegraph, in a multitude of flags, announced that ships, brigs, schooners, and steamers, in vast quantities, "were below." Nor was the peace alone the great feature of the holiday. The eighth of June, the natal day of Halifax, was to be celebrated also. For Halifax was founded, so says the Chronicle, on the eighth of June, 1749, by the Hon. Edward Cornwallis (not our Cornwallis), and the 'Alligonians in consequence made a specialty of that fact once a year. And to add to the attraction, the Board of Works had decided to lay the corner-stone of a Lunatic Asylum in the afternoon; so there was no end to the festivities. And, to crown all, an immense fog settled upon the city.

Leaning upon my friend Robert's arm and my staff, I went forth to see the grand review. When we arrived upon the ground, in the rear of Citadel Hill, we saw the outline of something glimmering through the fog, which Robert said were shrubs, and which I said were soldiers. A few minutes' walking proved my position to be correct; we found ourselves in the centre of a three-sided square of three regiments, within which the civic authorities were loyally boring Sir John Gaspard le Merchant and staff, to the verge of insanity, with the Address which was to be laid at the foot of the throne. Notwithstanding the despairing air with which His Excellency essayed to reply to this formidable paper, I could not help enjoying the scene; and I also noted, when the reply was over, and the few ragamuffins near His Excellency cheered bravely, and the band struck up the national anthem, how gravely and discreetly the rest of the 'Alligonians, in the circumambient fog, echoed the sentiment by a silence, that, under other circumstances, would have been disheartening. What a quiet people it is! As I said before, to make the festivities complete, in the afternoon there was a procession to lay the corner-stone of a Lunatic Asylum. But oh! how the jolly old rain poured down upon the luckless pilgrimage! There were the "Virgins" of Masonic Lodge No.—, the Army Masons, in scarlet; the African Masons, in ivory and black; the Scotch-piper Mason, with his legs in enormous plaid trowsers, defiant of Shakspeare's theory about the sensitiveness of some men, when the bag-pipe sings i' the nose; the Clerical Mason in shovel hat; the municipal artillery; the Sons of Temperance, and the band. Away they marched, with drum and banner, key and compasses, Bible and sword, to Dartmouth, in great feather, for the eyes of Halifax were upon them.

CHAPTER II.

Fog clears Up—The One Idea not comprehended by the American Mind—A June Morning in the Province—The Beginning of the Evangeliad—Intuitive Perception of Genius—The Forest Primeval—Acadian Peasants—A Negro Settlement—Deer's Castle—The Road to Chezzetcook—Acadian Scenery—A Glance at the Early History of Acadia—First Encroachments of the English—The Harbor and Village of Chezzetcook—Etc., etc.

The celebration being over, the fog cleared up. Loyalty furled her flags; the civic authorities were silent; the signal-telegraph was put upon short allowance. But the 'Alligonian papers next day were loaded to the muzzle with typographical missiles. From them we learned that there had been a great amount of enthusiasm displayed at the celebration, and "everything had passed off happily in spite of the weather." "Old Chebucto" was right side up, and then she quietly sparkled out again.

There is one solitary idea, and only one, not comprehensible by the American mind. I say it feebly, but I say it fearlessly, there is an idea which does not present anything to the American mind but a blank. Every metaphysical dog has worried the life out of every abstraction but this. I strike my stick down, cross my hands, and rest my chin upon them, in support of my position. Let anybody attempt to controvert it! "I say, that in the American mind, there is no such thing as the conception even, of an idea of tranquillity!" I once for a little repose, went to a "quiet New-England village," as it was called, and the first thing that attracted my attention there was a statement in the village paper, that no less than twenty persons in that quiet place had obtained patent-rights for inventions and improvements during the past year. They had been at everything, from an apple-parer to a steam-engine. In the next column was an article "on capital punishment," and the leader was thoroughly fired up with a bran-new project for a railroad to the Pacific. That day I dined with a member of Congress, a peripatetic lecturer, and the principal citizens of the township, and took the return cars at night amid the glare of a torch-light procession. Repose, forsooth? Why, the great busy city seemed to sing lullaby, after the shock of that quiet New-England village.

But in this quaint, mouldy old town, one can get an idea of the calm and the tranquil—especially after a celebration. It has been said: "Halifax is the only place that is finished." One can readily believe it. The population has been twenty-five thousand for the last twenty-five years, and a new house is beyond the memory of the oldest inhabitant.

The fog cleared up. And one of those inexpressibly balmy days followed. June in Halifax represents our early May. The trees are all in bud; the peas in the garden-beds are just marking the lines of drills with faint stripes of green. Here and there a solitary bird whets his bill on the bare bark of a forked bough. The chilly air has departed, and in its place is a sense of freshness, of dewiness, of fragrance and delight. A sense of these only, an instinctive feeling, that anticipates the odor of the rose before the rose is blown. On such a morning we went forth to visit Chezzetcook, and here, gentle reader, beginneth the Evangeliad.

The intuitive perception of genius is its most striking element. I was told by a traveller and an artist, who had been for nearly twenty years on the northwest coast, that he had read Irving's "Astoria" as a mere romance, in early life, but when he visited the place itself, he found that *he was reading the book over again*; that Irving's descriptions were so minute and perfect, that he was at home in Astoria, and familiar, not only with the country, but with individuals residing there; "for," said he, "although many of the old explorers, trappers, and adventurers described in the book were dead and gone, yet I found the descendants of those pioneers had the peculiar characteristics of their fathers; and the daughter of Concomly, whom I met, was as interesting a historical personage at home as Queen Elizabeth would have been in Westminster Abbey. At Vancouver's Island," said the traveller, "I found an old dingy copy of the book itself, embroidered and seamed with interlineations and marginal notes of hundreds of pens, in every style of chirography, yet all attesting the faithfulness of the narrative. I would have given anything for that copy, but I do not believe I could have purchased it with the price of the whole island."

What but that wonderful element of genius, *intuitive perception*, could have produced such a book? Irving was never on the Columbia River, never saw the northwest coast. "The materials were furnished him from the log-books and journals of the explorers themselves," says Dr. Dryasdust. True, my learned friend, but suppose I furnish you with pallet and colors, with canvas and brushes, the materials of art, will you paint me as I sit here, and make a living, breathing picture, that will survive my ashes for centuries? "I have not the genius of the artist," replies Dr. Dryasdust. Then, my dear Doctor, we will put the materials aside for the present, and venture a little farther with our theory of "intuitive perception."

Longfellow never saw the Acadian Land, and yet thus his pastoral begins:

"This is the forest primeval. The murmuring pines and the hemlocks."

This is the opening line of the poem: this is the striking feature of Nova Scotia scenery. The shores welcome us with waving masses of foliage, but not the foliage of familiar woods. As we travel on this hilly road to the Acadian settlement, we look up and say, "This is the forest primeval," but it is the forest of the poem, not that of our childhood. There is not, in all this vast greenwood, an oak, an elm, a chestnut, a beech, a cedar or maple. For miles and miles, we see nothing against the clear blue sky but the spiry tops of evergreens; or perhaps, a gigantic skeleton, "a rampike," pine or hemlock, scathed and spectral, stretches its gaunt outline above its fellows. Spruces and firs, such as adorn our gardens, cluster in never-ending profusion; and aromatic and unwonted odor pervades the air—the spicy breath of resinous balsams. Sometimes the sense is touched with a new fragrance, and presently we see a buckthorn, white with a thousand blossoms. These, however, only meet us at times. The distinct and characteristic feature of the forest is conveyed in that one line of the poet.

And yet another feature of the forest primeval presents itself, not less striking and unfamiliar. From the dead branches of those skeleton pines and hemlocks, these *rampikes*, hang masses of white moss, snow-white, amid the dark verdure. An actor might wear such a beard in the play of King Lear. Acadian children wore such to imitate "*grandpère*," centuries ago; Cowley's trees are "Patricians," these are Patriarchs.

——"the murmuring pines and the hemlocks, *Bearded with moss, and in garments green, indistinct in the twilight,Stand like Druids of old, with voices sad and prophetic,Stand like harpers hoar with beards that rest on their bosoms.*"

We are re-reading Evangeline line by line. And here, at this turn of the road, we encounter two Acadian peasants. The man wears an old tarpaulin hat, home-spun worsted shirt, and tarry canvas trowsers; innovation has certainly changed him, in costume at least, from the Acadian of our fancy; but the pretty brown-skinned girl beside him, with lustrous eyes, and soft black hair under her hood, with kirtle of antique form, and petticoat of holiday homespun, is true to tradition. There is nothing modern in the face or drapery of that figure. She might have stepped out of Normandy a century ago,

"Wearing her Norman cap, and her kirtle of blue, and the ear-ringsBrought in the olden time from France, and since, as an heir-loom,Handed down from mother to child, through long generations."

Alas! the ear-rings are worn out with age! but save them, the picture is very true to the life. As we salute the pair, we learn they have been walking on their way since dawn from distant Chezzetcook: the man speaks English with a strong French accent; the maiden only the language of her people on the banks of the Seine.

"Fair was she to behold, that maiden of seventeen summers, Black were her eyes as the berry that grows on the thorn by the way-side:Black, yet how softly they gleamed beneath the brown shade of her tresses."

Who can help repeating the familiar words of the idyl amid such scenery, and in such a presence?

"We are now approaching a Negro settlement," said my *compagnon de voyage* after we had passed the Acadians; "and we will take a fresh horse at Deer's Castle; this is rough travelling." In a few minutes we saw a log house perched on a bare bone of granite that stood out on a ragged hill-side, and presently another cabin of the same kind came in view. Then other scare-crow edifices wheeled in sight as we drove along; all forlorn, all patched with mud, all perched on barren knolls, or gigantic bars of granite, high up, like ragged redoubts of poverty, armed at every window with a formidable artillery of old hats, rolls of rags, quilts, carpets, and indescribable bundles, or barricaded with boards to keep out the air and sunshine.

"You do not mean to say those wretched hovels are occupied by living beings?" said I to my companion.

"Oh yes," he replied, with a quiet smile, "these are your people, your *fugitives*."

"But, surely," said I, "they do not live in those airy nests during your intensely cold winters?"

"Yes," replied my companion, "and they have a pretty hard time of it. Between you and I," he continued, "they are a miserable set of devils; they won't work, and they shiver it out here as well as they can. During the most of the year they are in a state of abject want, and then they are very humble. But in the strawberry season they make a little money, and while it lasts are fat and saucy enough. We can't do anything with them, they won't work. There they are in their cabins, just as you see them, a poor, woe-begone set of vagabonds; a burden upon the community; of no use to themselves, nor to anybody else."

"Ye who listen with credulity to the whispers of fancy and pursue with eagerness the phantoms of hope, who expect that age will perform the promises of youth, and that the deficiencies of the present day will be supplied by the morrow, attend to the history of Rasselas, here in his happy valley."

"Now then," said my companion, as this trite quotation was passing through my mind. The wagon had stopped in front of a little, weather-beaten house that kept watch and ward over an acre of greensward, broken ever and anon with a projecting bone of granite, and not only fenced with stone, but dotted also with various mounds of pebbles, some as large as a paving-stone, and some much larger. This was "Deer's Castle." In front of the castle was a swing-sign with an inscription:

"William Deer, who lives here, keeps the best of wine and beer, Brandy, and cider, and other good cheer; Fish, and ducks, and moose, and deer. Caught or shot in the woods just here, With cutlets, or steaks, as will appear; If you will stop you need not fear But you will be well treated by William Deer, And by Mrs. Deer, his dearest, deary dear!"

I quote from memory. The precise words have escaped me, but the above is the substance of the sense, and the metre is accurate.

It was a little, weather-beaten shanty of boards, that clung like flakes to the frame-work. A show-box of a room, papered with select wood-cuts from *Punch* and the *Illustrated London News*, was the grand banquet-hall of the castle. And indeed it was a castle compared with the wretched redoubts of poverty around it. Here we changed horses, or rather we exchanged our horse, for a diminutive, bantam pony, that, under the supervision of "Bill," was put inside the shafts and buckled up to the very roots of the harness. This Bill, the son and heir of the Castellen, was a good-natured yellow boy, about fifteen years of age, with such a development of under-lip and such a want of development elsewhere, that his head looked like a scoop. There was an infinite fund of humor in Billy, an uncontrollable sense of the comic, that would break out in spite of his grave endeavors to put himself under guard. It exhibited itself in his motions and gestures, in the flourish of his hands as he buckled up the pony, in the looseness of his gait, the swing of his head, and the roll of his eyes. His very language was pregnant with mirth; thus:

"Bill!"

"Cheh, cheh, sir? cheh."

"Is your father at home?"

"Cheh, cheh, father? cheh, cheh."

"Yes, your father?"

"Cheh, cheh, at home, sah? cheh."

"Yes, is your father at home?"

"I guess so, cheh, cheh."

"What is the matter with you, Bill? what are you laughing about?"

"Cheh, cheh, I don't know, sah, cheh, cheh."

"Well, take out the horse, and put in the pony; we want to go to Chizzencook."

"Cheh, Cheh'z'ncook? Yes, sah," and so with that facetious gait and droll twist of the elbow, Bill swings himself against the horse and unbuckles him in a perpetual jingle of merriment.

"And this," said I to my companion, as we looked from the door-step of the shanty upon the spiry tops of evergreens in the valley below us, and at the wretched log-huts that were roosting up on the bare rocks around us, "this is the negro settlement?"

"Yes," he replied.

"Are all the negro settlements in Nova Scotia as miserable, as this?"

"Yes," he answered; "you can tell a negro settlement at once by its appearance."

"Then," I thought to myself, "I would, for poor Cuffee's sake, that much-vaunted British sympathy and British philanthropy had something better to show to an admiring world than the prospect around Deer's Castle."

Notwithstanding the very generous banquet spread before the eyes of the traveller, on the sign-board, we were compelled to dismiss the pleasant fiction of the poet upon the announcement of Mrs. Deer, that "Nathin was in de house 'cept bacon," and she "reckoned" she "might have an egg or two by de time we got back from Chizzincook."

"But you have plenty of trout here in these streams?"

"Oh! yes, plenty, sah."

"Then let Bill catch some trout for us."

And so the pony being strapped up and buckled to the wagon, we left the negro settlement for the French settlement. They are all in "settlements," here, the people of this Province. Centuries are mutable, but prejudices never alter in the Colonies.

But we are again in the Acadian forest—a truce to moralizing—let us enjoy the scenery. The road we are on is but a few miles from the sea-shore, but the ocean is hidden from view by the thick woods. As we ride along, however, we skirt the edges of coves and inlets that frequently break in upon the landscape. There is a chain of fresh-water lakes also along this road; sometimes we cross a bridge over a rushing torrent; sometimes a calm expanse of water, doubling the evergreens at its margin, comes in view; anon a gleam of sapphire strikes through the verdure, and an ocean-bay with its shingly beach curves in and out between the piny slopes. At last we reach the crest of a hill, and at the foot of the road is another bridge, a house, a wharf, and two or three coasters at anchor in a diminutive harbor. This is "Three Fathom Harbor." We are within a mile of Chezzetcook.

Now if it were not for Pony we should press on to the settlement, but we must give Pony a respite. Pony is an enthusiastic little fellow, but his lungs are too much for him, they have blown him out like a bagpipe. A mile farther and then eleven miles back to Deer's Castle, is a great undertaking for so small an animal. In the meanwhile, we will ourselves rest and take some "home-brewed" with the landlord, who is harbor-master, inn-keeper, store-keeper, fisherman, shipper, skipper, mayor, and corporation of Three Fathom Harbor, beside being father of the town, for all the children in it are his own. A draught of foaming ale, a whiff or two from a clay pipe, a look out of the window to be assured that Pony had subsided, and we take leave of the corporate authority of Three Fathom Harbor, and are once more on the road.

One can scarcely draw near to a settlement of these poor refugees without a feeling of pity for the sufferings they have endured; and this spark of pity quickly warms and kindles into indignation when we think of the story of hapless Acadia—the grievous wrong done those simple-minded, harmless, honest people, by the rapacious, free-booting adventurers of merry England, and those precious filibusters, our Pilgrim Fathers.

The early explorations of the French in the young hemisphere which Columbus had revealed to the older half of the world, have been almost entirely obscured by the greater events which followed. Nearly a century after the first colonies were established in New France, New England was discovered. I shall not dwell upon the importance of this event, as it has been so often alluded to by historians and others; and, indeed, I believe it is generally acknowledged now, that the finding of the continent itself would have been a failure had it not been for the discovery of Massachusetts. As this, however, happened long after the establishment of Acadia, and as the Pilgrim Fathers did not interfere with their French neighbors for a surprising length of time, it will be as well not to expatiate upon it at present. In the course of a couple of centuries or so, I shall have occasion to allude to it, in connection with the story of the neutral French.

In the year 1504, says the Chronicle, some fishermen from Brittany discovered the island that now forms the eastern division of Nova Scotia, and named it "Cape Breton." Two years after, Dennys of Harfleur, made a rude chart of the vast sheet of water that stretches from Cape Breton and Newfoundland to the mainland. In 1534, Cartier, sailing under the orders of the French Admiral, Chabot, visited the coast of Newfoundland, crossed the gulf Dennys had seen and described twenty-eight years before, and took possession of the country around it, in the name of the king, his master. As Cartier was recrossing the Gulf, on his return voyage, he named the waters he was sailing upon "St. Lawrence," in honor of that saint whose day chanced to turn up on the calendar at that very happy time. According to some accounts, Baron de Lery established a settlement here as early as 1518. Some authorities state that a French colony was planted on the St. Lawrence as early as 1524, and soon after others were formed in Canada and Nova Scotia. In 1535, Cartier again crossed the waters of the Gulf, and following the course of the river, penetrated into the interior until he reached an island upon which was a hill; this he named "*Mont Real*." Various adventurers followed these first discoverers and explorers, and the coast was from time to time visited by French ships, in pursuit of the fisheries.

Among these expeditions, one of the most eminent was that of Champlain, who, in the year 1609, penetrated as far south as the head waters of the Hudson River; visited Lake George and the cascades of Ticonderoga; and gave his own name to the lake which lies between the proud shores of New York and New England. Thence le Sr. Champlain, "*Capitaine pour le Roy*," travelled westward, as far as the country of the Hurons, giving to the discovered territory the title of Nouvelle France; and to the lakes Ontario, Erie, and Huron, the names of St. Louis, Mer Douce, and

Grand Lac; which any person can see by referring to the original chart in the State library of New York. But before these discoveries of Champlain, an important step had been taken by the parent government. In the year 1603, an expedition, under the patronage of Henry IV., sailed for the New World. The leader of this was a Protestant gentleman, by name De Monts. As the people under his command were both Protestants and Catholics, De Monts had permission given in his charter to establish, as one of the fundamental laws of the Colony, the free exercise of "religious worship," upon condition of settling in the country, and teaching the Roman Catholic faith to the savages. Heretofore, all the countries discovered by the French had been called New France, but in De Monts' Patent, that portion of the territory lying east of the Penobscot and embracing the present provinces of New Brunswick, Nova Scotia, and part of Maine was named "Acadia."

The little colony under De Monts flourished in spite of the rigors of the climate, and its commander, with a few men, explored the coast on the St. Lawrence and the bay of Fundy, as well as the rivers of Maine, the Penobscot, the Kennebec, the Saco and Casco Bay, and even coasted as far south as the long, hook-shaped cape that is now known in all parts of the world as the famous Cape Cod. In a few years, the settlement began to assume a smiling aspect; houses were erected, and lands were tilled; the settlers planted seeds and gathered the increase thereof; gardens sprang out of the wilderness, peace and order reigned everywhere, and the savage tribes around viewed the kind, light-hearted colonists with admiration and fraternal good-will. It is pleasant to read this part of the chronicle—of their social meetings in the winter at the banqueting hall; of the order of "*Le Bon Temps*," established by Champlain; of the great pomp and insignia of office (a collar, a napkin, and staff) of the grand chamberlain, whose government only lasted for a day, when he was supplanted by another; of their dinners in the sunshine amid the corn-fields; of their boats, banners, and music on the water; of their gentleness, simplicity, and honest, hearty enjoyments. These halcyon days soon came to an end. The infamous Captain Argall, hearing that a number of white people had settled in this hyperborean region, set sail from Jamestown for the colony, in a ship of fourteen guns, in the midst of a profound peace, to burn, pillage, and slaughter the intruders upon the territory of Virginia! Finding the people unprepared for defence, his enterprise was successful. Argall took possession of the lands, in the name of the King of England, laid waste some of the settlements, burned the forts, and, under circumstances of peculiar perfidy, induced a number of the poor Acadians to go with him to Jamestown. Here they were treated as pirates, thrown into prison, and sentenced to be executed. Argall, who it seems had some touch of manhood in his nature, upon this confessed to the Governor, Sir Thomas Dale, that these people had a patent from the King of France, which he had stolen from them and concealed, and that they were not pirates, but simply colonists. Upon this, Sir Thomas Dale was induced to fit out an expedition to dislodge the rest of them from Acadia. Three ships were got ready, the brave Captain Argall was appointed Commander-in-chief, and the first colony was terminated by fire and sword before the end of the year. This was in 1613, ten years after the first planting of Acadia.

"Some of the settlers," says the Chronicle, "finding resistance to be unavailing, fled to the woods." What became of them history does not inform us, but with a graceful appearance of candor, relates that the transaction itself "was not approved of by the court of England, nor resented by that of France." Five years afterward we find Captain Argall appointed Deputy-Governor of Virginia.

This outrage was the initial letter only of a series that for nearly a century and a half after, made the successive colonists of Acadia the prey of their rapacious neighbors. We shall take up the story from time to time, gentle reader, as we voyage around and through the province. Meanwhile let us open our eyes again upon the present, for just below us lies the village and harbor of Chezzetcook.

A conspiracy of earth and air and ocean had certainly broken out that morning, for the ominous lines of Fog and Mist were hovering afar off upon the boundaries of the horizon. Under the crystalline azure of a summer sky, the water of the harbor had an intensity of color rarely seen, except in the pictures of the most ultra-marine painters. Here and there a green island or a fishing-boat rested upon the surface of the tranquil blue. For miles and miles the eye followed indented grassy slopes, that rolled away on either side of the harbor, and the most delicate pencil could scarcely portray the exquisite line of creamy sand that skirted their edges and melted off in the clear margin of the water. Occasional little cottages nestle among these green banks, not the Acadian houses of the poem, "with thatched roofs, and dormer windows projecting," but comfortable, homely-looking buildings of modern shapes, shingled and un-weather-cocked. No cattle visible, no ploughs nor horses. Some of the men are at work in the open air; all in tarpaulin hats, all in tarry canvas trowsers. These are boat-builders and coopers. Simple, honest, and good-tempered enough; you see how courteously they salute us as we ride by them. In front of every house there is a knot of curious little faces; Young Acadia is out this bright day, and although Young Acadia has not a clean face on, yet its hair is of the darkest and softest, and its eyes are lustrous and most delicately fringed. Yonder is one of the veterans of the place, so we will tie Pony to the fence, and rest here.

"Fine day you have here," said my companion.

"Oh yes! oh yes!" (with great deference and politeness).

"Can you give us anything in the way of refreshment? a glass of ale, or a glass of milk?"

"Oh no!" (with the unmistakable shrug of the shoulders); "we no have milk, no have ale, no have brandy, no have noting here: ah! we very poor peep' here." (Poor people here.)

"Can we sit down and rest in one of your houses?"

"Oh yes! oh yes!" (with great politeness and alacrity); "walk in, walk in; we very poor peep', no milk, no brandy: walk in."

The little house is divided by a partition. The larger half is the hall, the parlor, kitchen, and nursery in one. A huge fire-place, an antique spinning-wheel, a bench, and two settles, or high-backed seats, a table, a cradle and a baby very wide awake, complete the inventory. In the apartment adjoining is a bin that represents, no doubt, a French bedstead of the early ages. Everything is suggestive of boat-builders, of Robinson Crusoe work, of undisciplined hands, that have had to do with ineffectual tools. As you look at the walls, you see the house is built of timbers, squared and notched together, and caulked with moss or oakum.

"Very poor peep' here," says the old man, with every finger on his hands stretched out to deprecate the fact. By the fire-side sits an old woman, in a face all cracked and seamed with wrinkles, like a picture by one of the old masters. "Yes," she echoes, "very poor peep' here, and very cold, too, sometime." By this time the door-way is entirely packed with little, black, shining heads, and curious faces, all shy, timid, and yet not the less good-natured. Just back of the cradle are two of the Acadian women, "knitters i' the sun," with features that might serve for Palmer's sculptures; and eyes so lustrous, and teeth so white, and cheeks so rich with brown and blush, that if one were a painter and not an invalid, he might pray for canvas and pallet as the very things most wanted in the critical moment of his life. Faed's picture does not convey the Acadian face. The mouth and chin are more delicate in the real than in the ideal Evangeline. If you look again, after the first surprise is over, you will see that these are the traditional pictures, such as we might have fancied they should be, after reading the idyl. From the forehead of each you see at a glance how the dark mass of hair has been combed forward and over the face, that the little triangular Norman cap might be tied across the crown of the head. Then the hair is thrown back again over this, so as to form a large bow in front, then re-tied at the crown with colored ribbons. Then you see it has been plaited in a shining mesh, brought

46

forward again, and braided with ribbons, so that it forms, as it were, a pretty coronet, well-placed above those brilliant eyes and harmonious features. This, with the antique kirtle and picturesque petticoat, is an Acadian portrait. Such is it now, and such it was, no doubt, when De Monts sailed from Havre de Grace, two centuries and a half ago. In visiting this kind and simple people, one can scarcely forget the little chapel. The young French priest was in his garden, behind the little tenement, set apart for him by the piety of his flock, and readily admitted us. A small place indeed was it, but clean and orderly, the altar decorated with toy images, that were not too large for a Christmas table. Yet I have been in the grandest tabernacles of episcopacy with lesser feelings of respect than those which were awakened in that tiny Acadian chapel. Peace be with it, and with its gentle flock.

"Pony is getting impatient," said my companion, as we reverently stepped from the door-way, "and it is a long ride to Halifax." So, with courteous salutation on both sides, we take leave of the good father, and once more are on the road to Deer's Castle.

CHAPTER III.

A Romp at Three Fathom Harbor—The Moral Condition of the Acadians—The Wild Flowers of Nova Scotia—Mrs. Deer's Wit—No Fish—Picton—The Balaklava Schooner—And a Voyage to Louisburgh.

Pony is very enterprising. We are soon at the top of the first long hill, and look again, for the last time, upon the Acadian village. How cosily and quietly it is nestled down amid those graceful green slopes! What a bit of poetry it is in itself! Jog on, Pony!

The corporate authority of Three Fathom Harbor has been improving his time during our absence. As we drive up we find him in high romp with a brace of buxom, red-cheeked, Nova Scotia girls, who have just alighted from a wagon. The landlady of Three Fathom Harbor, in her matronly cap, is smiling over the little garden gate at her lord, who is pursuing his Daphnes, and catching, and kissing, and hugging, first one and then the other, to his heart's content. Notwithstanding their screams, and slaps, and robust struggles, it is very plain to be seen that the skipper's attentions are not very unwelcome. Leaving his fair friends, he catches Pony by the bridle and stops us with a hospitable—"Come in—you must come in; just a glass of ale, you'll want it;" and sure enough, we found when we came to taste the ale, that we did want it, and many thanks to him, the kind-hearted landlord of the Three Fathoms.

"It is surprising," said I to my companion, as we rolled again over the road, "that these people, these Acadians, should still preserve their language and customs, so near to your principal city, and yet with no more affiliation than if they were on an island in the South Seas!"

"The reason of that," he replied, "is because they stick to their own settlement; never see anything of the world except Halifax early in the morning; never marry out of their own set; never read—I do not believe one of them can read or write—and are in fact *so slow*, so destitute of enterprise, so much behind the age"——

I could not avoid smiling. My companion observed it. "What are you thinking about?" said he.

The truth is, I was thinking of Halifax, which was anything but a *fast* place; but I simply observed:

"Your settlements here are somewhat novel to a stranger. That a mere handful of men should be so near your city, and yet so isolated: that this village of a few hundred only, should retain its customs and language, intact, for generation after generation, within walking distance of Halifax, seems to me unaccountable. But let me ask you," I continued, "what is the moral condition of the Acadians?"

"As for that," said he, "I believe it stands pretty fair. I do not think an Acadian would cheat, lie, or steal; I know that the women are virtuous, and if I had a thousand pounds in my pocket I could sleep with confidence in any of their houses, although all the doors were unlocked and everybody in the village knew it."

"That," said I, "reminds one of the poem:

'Neither locks had they to their doors, nor bars to their windows,But their dwellings were open as day and the hearts of their owners;There the richest was poor, and the poorest lived in abundance.'"

Poor exiles! You will never see the Gasperau and the shore of the Basin of Minas, but if this very feeble life I have holds out, I hope to visit Grandpré and the broad meadows that gave a name to the village.

One thing Longfellow has certainly omitted in "Evangeline"—the wild flowers of Acadia. The roadside is all fringed and tasselled with white, pink, and purple. The wild strawberries are in blossom, whitening the turf all the way from Halifax to Chezzetcook. You see their starry settlements thick in every bit of turf. These are the silver mines of poor Cuffee; he has the monopoly of the berry trade. It is his only revenue. Then in the swampy grounds there are long green needles in solitary groups, surmounted with snowy tufts; and here and there, clusters of light purple blossoms, called laurel flowers, but not like our laurels, spring up from the bases of grey rocks and boulders; sometimes a rich array of blood-red berries gleams out of a mass of greenery; then again great floral white radii, tipped with snowy petals, rise up profuse and lofty; down by the ditches hundreds of pitcher plants lift their veined and mottled vases, brimming with water, to the wood-birds who drink and perch upon their thick rims; May-flowers of delightful fragrance hide beneath those shining, tropical-looking leaves, and meadow-sweet, not less fragrant, but less beautiful, pours its tender aroma into the fresh air; here again we see the buckthorn in blossom; there, scattered on the turf, the scarlet partridge berry; then wild-cherry trees, mere shrubs only, in full bud; and around all and above all, the evergreens, the murmuring pines, and the hemlocks; the rampikes—the grey-beards of the primeval forest; the spicy breath of resinous balsams; the spiry tops, and the serene heaven. Is this fairy land? No, it is only poor, old, barren Nova Scotia, and yet I think Felix, Prince of Salerno, if he were here, might say, and say truly too, "In all my life I never beheld a more enchanting place;" but Felix, Prince of Salerno, must remember this is the month of June, and summer is not perpetual in the latitude of forty-five.

We reach at last Deer's Castle. Pony, under the hands of Bill, seems remarkably cheerful and fresh after his long travel up hill and down. When he pops out of his harness, with his knock-knees and sturdy, stocky little frame, he looks very like an animated saw-buck, clothed in seal-skin; and with a jump, and snort, and flourish of tail, he escorts Bill to the stable, as if twenty miles over a rough road was a trifle not worth consideration.

A savory odor of frying bacon and eggs stole forth from the door as we sat, in the calm summer air, upon the stone fence. William Deer, Jr., was wandering about in front of the castle, endeavoring to get control of his under lip and keep his exuberant mirth within the limits of decorum; but every instant, to use a military figure, it would flash in the pan. Up on the bare rocks were the wretched, woe-begone, patched, and ragged log huts of poor Cuffee. The hour and the season were suggestive of philosophizing, of theories, and questions.

"Mrs. Deer," said I, "is that your husband's portrait on the back of the sign?" (there was a picture of a stag with antlers on the reverse of the poetical swing-board, either intended as a pictographic pun upon the name of "Deer," or as a hint to sportsmen of good game hereabouts).

"Why," replied Mrs. Deer, an old tidy wench, of fifty, pretty well bent by rheumatism, and so square in the lower half of her figure, and so spare in the upper, that she appeared to have been carved out of her own hips: "why, as to dat, he ain't good-looking to brag on, but I don't think he looks quite like a beast neither."

At this unexpected retort, Bill flashed off so many pans at once that he seemed to be a platoon of militia. My companion also enjoyed it immensely. Being an invalid, I could not participate in the general mirth.

"Mrs. Deer," said I, "how long have you lived here?"

"Oh, sah! a good many years; I cum here afore I had Bill dar." (Here William flashed in the pan twice.)

"Where did you reside before you came to Nova Scotia?"

"Sah?"

"Where did you live?"

"Oh, sah! I is from Maryland." (William at it again.)

"Did you run away?"

"Yes, sah; I left when I was young. Bill, what you laughing at? I was young once."

"Were you married then—when you run away?"

"Oh yes, sah!" (a glance at Bill, who was off again).

"And left your husband behind in Maryland?"

"Yes, sah; but he didn't stay long dar after I left. He was after me putty sharp, soon as I travelled;" (here Mrs. Deer and William interchanged glances, and indulged freely in mirth).

"And which place do you like the best—this or Maryland?"

"Why, I never had no such work to do at home as I have to do here, grubbin' up old stumps and stones; dem isn't women's work. When I was home, I had only to wait on misses, and work was light and easy." (William quiet.)

"But which place do you like the best—Nova Scotia or Maryland?"

"Oh! de work here is awful, grubbin' up old stones and stumps; 'tain't fit for women." (William much impressed with the cogency of this repetition.)

"But which place do you like the best?"

"And de winter here, oh! it's wonderful tryin." (William utters an affirmative flash.)

"But which place do you like the best?"

"And den dere's de rheumatiz."

"But which place do you like the best, Mrs. Deer?"

"Well," said Mrs. Deer, glancing at Bill, "I like Nova Scotia best." (Whatever visions of Maryland were gleaming in William's mind, seemed to be entirely quenched by this remark.)

"But why," said I, "do you prefer Nova Scotia to Maryland? Here you have to work so much harder, to suffer so much from the cold and the rheumatism, and get so little for it;" for I could not help looking over the green patch of stony grass that has been rescued by the labor of a quarter century.

"Oh!" replied Mrs. Deer, "de difference is, dat when I work here, I work for myself, and when I was working at home, I was working for other people." (At this, William broke forth again in such a series of platoon flashes, that we all joined in with infinite merriment.)

"Mrs. Deer," said I, recovering my gravity, "I want to ask you one more question."

"Well, sah," said the lady Deer, cocking her head on one side, expressive of being able to answer any number of questions in a twinkling.

"You have, no doubt, still many relatives left in Maryland?"

"Oh! yes," replied Mrs. Deer, "*all* of dem are dar."

"And suppose you had a chance to advise them in regard to this matter, would you tell them to run away, and take their part with you in Nova Scotia, or would you advise them to stay where they are?"

Mrs. Deer, at this, looked a long time at William, and William looked earnestly at his parent. Then she cocked her head on the other side, to take a new view of the question. Then she gathered up mouth and eyebrows, in a puzzle, and again broadened out upon Bill in an odd kind of smile; at last she doubled up one fist, put it against her cheek, glanced at Bill, and out came the answer: "Well, sah, I'd let 'em take dere own heads for dat!" I must confess the philosophy of this remark awakened in me a train of very grave reflections; but my companion burst into a most obstreperous laugh. As for Mrs. Deer, she shook her old hips as long as she could stand, and then sat down and continued, until she wiped the tears out of her eyes with the corner of her apron. William cast himself down upon a strawberry bank, and gave way to the most flagrant mirth, kicking up his old shoes in the air, and fairly wallowing in laughter and blossoms. I endeavored to change the subject. "Bill, did you catch any trout?" It was some time before William could control himself enough to say, "Not a single one, sah;" and then he rolled over on his back, put his black paws up to his eyes, and twitched and jingled to his heart's content. I did not ask Mrs. Deer any more questions; but there is a moral in the story, enough for a day.

As we rattled over the road, after our brief dinner at Deer's Castle, I could not avoid a pervading feeling of gloom and disappointment, in spite of the balmy air and pretty landscape. The old ragged abodes of wretchedness seemed to be too clearly defined—to stand out too intrusively against the bright blue sky. But why should I feel so much for Cuffee? Has he not enlisted in his behalf every philanthropist in England? Is he not within ten miles of either the British flag or Acadia? Does not the Duchess of Sutherland entertain the authoress of Uncle Tom's Cabin, and the Black Swan? Why should I sorrow for Cuffee, when he is in the midst of his best friends? Why should I pretend to say that this appears to be the raggedest, the meanest, the worst condition of humanity, when the papers are constantly lauding British philanthropy, and holding it up as a great example, which we must "bow down and worship?" For my own part, although the pleasant fiction of seeing Cuffee clothed, educated, and Christianized, seemed to be somewhat obscured in this glimpse of his real condition, yet I hope he will do well under his new owners; at the very least, I trust his berry crop will be good, and that a benevolent British blanket or two may enable him to shiver out the winter safely, if not comfortably. Poor William Deer, Sen'r, of Deer's Castle, was suffering with rheumatism in the next apartment, while we were at his eggs and bacon in the banquet hall; but Deer of Deer's Castle is a prince to his neighbors. I shall not easily forget the brightening eye, the swift glance of intelligence in the face of another old negro, an hostler, in Nova Scotia. He was from Virginia, and adopting the sweet, mellifluous language of his own home, I asked him whether he liked best to stay where he was, or go back to "Old Virginny?" "O massa!" said he, with such a look, "you must know dat I has de warmest side for my own country!"

We rattled soberly into Dartmouth, and took the ferry-boat across the bay to the city. At the hotel there was no little questioning about Chezzetcook, for some of the Halifax merchants are at the Waverley. "Goed bless ye, what took ye to Chizzencook?" said one, "I never was there een in my life; ther's no bizz'ness ther, noathing to be seen: ai doant think there is a maen in Halifax scairsly, 'as ever seen the place."

At the supper-table, while we were discussing, over the cheese and ale, the Chezzetcook and negro settlements, and exhibiting with no little vainglory a gorgeous bunch of wild flowers (half of which vanity my *compagnon de voyage* is accountable for), there was a young English-Irish gentleman, well built, well featured, well educated: by name—I shall call him Picton.

Picton took much interest in Deer's Castle and Chezzetcook, but slily and satirically. I do not think this the best way for a young man to begin with; but nevertheless, Picton managed so well to keep his sarcasms within the bounds of good humor, that before eleven o'clock we had become pretty well acquainted. At eleven o'clock the gas is turned off at Hotel Waverley. We went to bed, and renewed the acquaintance at breakfast. Picton had travelled overland from Montreal to take the "Canada" for Liverpool, and had arrived too late. Picton had nearly a fortnight before him in which to anticipate the next steamer. Picton was terribly bored with Halifax. Picton wanted to go somewhere—where?—"he did not care where." The consequence was a consultation upon the best disposal of a fortnight of waste time, a general survey of the maritime craft of Halifax, the selection of the schooner "Balaklava," bound for Sydney in ballast, and an understanding with the captain, that the old French town of Louisburgh was the point we wished to arrive at, into which harbor we expected to be put safely—three hundred and odd miles from Halifax, and this side of Sydney about sixty-two miles by sea. To all this did captain Capstan "seriously incline," and the result was, two berths in the "Balaklava," several cans of preserved meats and soups, a hamper of ale, two bottles of Scotch whisky, a ramshackle, Halifax van for the luggage, a general shaking of hands at departure, and another set of white sails among the many white sails in the blue harbor of Chebucto.

The "Balaklava" glimmered out of the harbor. Slowly and gently we swept past the islands and great ships; there on the shore is Point Pleasant in full uniform, its red soldiers and yellow tents in the thick of the pines and spruces; yonder is the admiralty, and the "Boscawen" seventy-four, the receiving-ship, a French war-steamer, and merchantmen of all flags. Slowly and gently we swept out past the round fort and long barracks, past the lighthouse and beaches, out upon the tranquil ocean, with its ominous fog-banks on the skirts of the horizon; out upon the evening sea, with the summer air fanning our faces, and a large white Acadian moon, faintly defined overhead.

Picton was a traveller; anybody could see that he was a traveller, and if he had then been in any part of the habitable globe, in Scotland or Tartary, Peru or Pennsylvania, there would not have been the least doubt about the fact that he was a traveller travelling on his travels. He looked like a traveller, and was dressed like a traveller. He had a travelling-cap, a travelling-coat, a portable-desk, a life-preserver, a water-proof blanket, a travelling-shirt, a travelling green leather satchel strapped across his shoulder, a Minié-rifle, several trunks adorned with geographical railway labels of all colors and languages, cork-soled boots, a pocket-compass, and a hand-organ. As for the hand-organ, that was an accident in his outfit. The hand-organ was a present for a little boy on the other side of the ocean; but nevertheless, it played its part very pleasantly in the cabin of the "Balaklava." And now let me observe here, that when we left Halifax in the schooner, I was scarcely less feeble than when I left New York. I mention it to show how speedily "roughing it" on the salt water will bring one's stomach to its senses.

The "Balaklava" was a fore-and-aft schooner in ballast, and very little ballast at that; easily handled; painted black outside, and pink inside; as staunch a craft as ever shook sail; very obedient to the rudder; of some seventy or eighty tons burden; clean and neat everywhere, except in the cabin. As for her commander, he was a fine gentleman; true, honest, brave, modest, prudent and courteous. Sincerely polite, for if politeness be only kindness mixed with refinement, then Captain Capstan was polite, as we understand it. The mate of the schooner was a cannie Scot; by name, Robert, Fitzjames, Buchanan, Wallace, Burns, Bruce; and Bruce was as jolly a first-mate as ever sailed under the cross-bones of the British flag. The crew was composed of four Newfoundland sailor men; and the cook, whose h'eighth letter of the h'alphabet smacked somewhat strongly of H'albion. As for the rest, there was Mrs. Captain Capstan, Captain and Mrs. Captain Capstan's baby; Picton and myself. It is cruel to speak of a baby, except in terms of endearment and affection, and therefore I could not but condemn Picton, who would sometimes, in his position as a traveller, allude to baby in language of most emphatic character. The fact is, Picton *swore* at that baby! Baby was in feeble health and would sometimes bewail its fate as if the cabin of the "Balaklava" were four times the size of baby's misfortunes. So Picton got to be very nervous and uncharitable, and slept on deck after the first night.

"How do you like this?" said Picton, as we leaned over the side of the "Balaklava," looking down at the millions of gelatinous quarls in the clear waters.

"Oh! very much; this lazy life will soon bring me up; how exhilarating the air is—how fresh and free!

"'A life on the ocean wave, A home on the rolling deep.'"

Just then the schooner gave a lurch and shook her feathers alow and aloft by way of chorus. "I like this kind of life very much; how gracefully this vessel moves; what a beautiful union of strength, proportion, lightness, in the taper masts, the slender ropes and stays, the full spread and sweep of her sails! Then how expansive the view, the calm ocean in its solitude, the receding land, the twinkling lighthouse, the"——

"Ever been sea-sick?" said Picton, drily.

"Not often. By the way, my appetite is improving; I think Cookey is getting tea ready, by the smoke and the smell."

"Likely," replied Picton; "let us take a squint at the galley."

To the galley we went, where we saw Cookey in great distress; for the wind would blow in at the wrong end of his stove-pipe, so as to reverse the draft, and his stove was smoking at every seam. Poor Cookey's eyes were full of tears.

"Why don't you turn the elbow of the pipe the other way?" said Picton.

"Hi av tried that," said Cookey, "but the helbow is so 'eavy the 'ole thing comes h'off."

"Then, take off the elbow," said Picton.

So Cookey did, and very soon tea was ready. Imagine a cabin, not much larger than a good-sized omnibus, and far less steady in its motion, choked up with trunks, and a table about the size of a wash-stand; imagine two stools and a locker to sit on: a canvas table-cloth in full blotch; three chipped yellow mugs by way of cups; as many plates, but of great variety of gap, crack, and pattern; pewter spoons; a blacking-bottle of milk; an earthen piggin of brown sugar, embroidered with a lively gang of great, fat, black pismires; hard bread, old as Nineveh; and butter of a most forbidding aspect. Imagine this array set before an invalid, with an appetite of the most Miss Nancyish kind!

"One misses the comforts here at sea," said the captain's lady, a pretty young woman, with a sweet Milesian accent.

"Yes, ma'am," said I, glancing again at the banquet.

"I don't rightly know," she continued, "how I forgot the rocking-chair;" and she gave baby an affectionate squeeze.

"And that," said the captain, "is as bad as me forgetting the potatoes."

Pic and I sat down, but we could neither eat nor drink; we were very soon on deck again, sucking away dolefully at two precious cigars. At last he broke out:

"By gad, to think of it!"

"What is the matter?" said I.

"Not a potato on board the 'Balaklava!'"

So we pulled away dolefully at our segars, in solemn silence.

"Picton," said I, "did you ever hear 'Annie Laurie?'"

"Yes," replied Picton, "about as many times as I want to hear it."

"Don't be impolite, Picton," said I; "it is not my intention to sing it this evening. Indeed, I never heard it before I heard it in Halifax. I had the good fortune to make one of a very pleasant company, at the house of an old friend in the city, and I must say that song touched me, both the song and the *singing* of it. You know it was *the* song in the Crimea?"

"Yes," said Picton, smoking vigorously.

"I asked Major ——," said I, "if 'Annie Laurie' was sung by the soldiers in the Crimea; and he replied 'they did not sing anything else; they sang it,' said he, 'by thousands at a time.' How does it go, Picton? Come now!"

So Picton held forth under the moon, and sang "Annie Laurie" on the "Balaklava." And long after we turned in, the music kept singing on—

"Her voice is low and sweet, And she's all the world to me; And for bonnie Annie Laurie I'd lay me down and dee."

CHAPTER IV.

The Voyage of the "Balaklava"—Something of a Fog—A Novel Sensation—Picton bursts out—"Nothing to do"—Breakfast under Way—A Phantom Boat—Mackerel—Gone, Hook and Line—The Colonists—Sectionalism and Prejudices—Cod-fishing and an Unexpected Banquet—Past the Old French Town—A Pretty Respectable Breeze—We get past the Rocks—Louisburgh.

"Picton!"

"Hallo!" replied the traveller, sitting up on his locker; "what is the matter now?"

"Nothing, only it is morning; let us get up, I want to see the sun rise out of the ocean."

"Pooh!" replied Picton, "what do you want to be bothering with the sun for?" And again Picton rolled himself up in his sheet-rubber travelling-blanket, and stretched his long body out on the locker. I got up, or rather got down, from my berth, and casting a bucket over the schooner's side soon made a sea-water toilet. I forgot to mention the sleeping arrangements of the "Balaklava." There were two lower berths on one side the cabin, either of which was large enough for two persons; and two single upper berths on the other side, neither of which was large enough for one person. At the proper hour for retiring, the captain's lady shut the cabin-door to keep out intruders, deliberately arrayed herself in dimity, turned in with baby in one of the large berths, and reöpened the door. There she lay, wide awake, with her bright eyes twinkling within the folds of her night cap, unaffected, chatty, and agreeable; then

64

the captain divested himself of boots and pea-jacket and turned in beside his lady (the mate slept, when off his watch, in the other double berth). Picton rolled himself up in his blanket and stretched out on his locker; I climbed into the narrow coop, over the salt beef and hard biscuit department; and so we dozed and talked until sleep reigned over all. In the morning the ceremonies were reversed, with the exception of the Captain, who was up first. "I never see a man sleep so little as the captain," said Bruce; "about two hoors, an' that's aw."

The sun was already risen when I came out on the deck of the "Balaklava;" but where was the sun? Indeed, where was the ocean, or anything? The schooner was barely making steerage-way, with a light head-wind, over a small patch of water, not much larger apparently than the schooner herself. The air was filled with a luminous haze that appeared to be penetrable by the eye, and yet was not; that seemed at once open and dense; near yet afar off; close yet diffuse; contracted yet boundless. There was no light nor shade, no outline, distance, aërial perspective. There was no east and west, nor blushing Aurora, rising from old Tithonus' bed; nor blue sky, nor green sea, nor ship, nor shore, nor color, tint, hue, ray, or reflection. There was nothing visible except the sides of the vessel, a maze of dripping rigging, two sailors bristling with drops, and the captain in a shiny sou-wester. The feeling of seclusion and security was complete, although we might have been run down by another vessel at any moment; the air was deliciously bland, invigorating, and pregnant with life; to breathe it was a transport; you felt it in every globule of blood, in every pore of the lungs. I could have hugged that fog, I was so happy!

Up and down the rolling deck I marched, and with every inspiration of the moist air, felt the old, tiresome, lingering sickness floating away. Then I was startled with a new sensation, I began to get hungry!

It was between four and five o'clock in the morning, and the "Balaklava" did not breakfast until eight. Reader, were you ever hungry *at sea*? Were you ever on deck, upon the measureless ocean, four hours earlier than the ring of the breakfast-bell? Were you ever awake on the briny deep, in advance, when the cook had yet two hours to sleep; when the stove in the galley was cold, and the kindling-wood unsplit; the coffee still in its tender, green, unroasted innocence? Were you ever upon "the blue, the fresh, the ever free," under these circumstances? If so, I need not say to *you* that the sentiment, then and there awakened, is stronger than avarice, pride, ambition or, love.

Presently Picton burst out like a flower on deck, in a mass of over-coats, with an India-rubber mackintosh by way of calyx. These were his night-clothes. Picton could do nothing except in full costume; he could not fish, in ever so small a stream, without being booted to the hips; nor shoot, in ever so good a cover, without being jacketed above the hips. He shaved himself in front of a silver-mounted dressing-case, wrote his letters on a portable secretary, drew off his boots with a patent boot-jack, brewed his punch with a peripatetic kettle, and in fact carried a little London with him in every quarter of the globe. "Well," said Picton, looking around at the fog with a low and expressive whistle, "this *is* serene!"

Although Picton used the word "serene" ironically, just as a man riding in an omnibus and suddenly discovering that he was destitute of the needful sixpence might exclaim, "This is pleasant," yet the phrase was not out of place. The "Balaklava" was gliding lazily over the water, at the rate of three knots an hour, sometimes giving a little lurch by way of shaking the wet out of her invisible sails, for the fog obscured all her upper canvas, and the mind and body easily yielded to the lullaby movement of the vessel. Talk of lotus-eating; of Castles of Indolence; of the dreamy ether inhaled from amber-tubed narghilé; of poppy and mandragora, and all the drowsy syrups of the world; of rain upon the midnight roof; the cooing of doves, the hush of falling snow, the murmur of brooks, the long summer song of grasshoppers in the field, the tinkling of fountains, and everything else that can soothe, lull, or tranquillize; and what are these to the serenity of this sail-swinging, ripple-stirring, gently-creaking craft, in her veil of luminous vapor? "How delightful this is!" said I.

The traveller eyed me with surprise, but at last comprehending the idea, admitted, that with the exception of the fog and the calm, the scarcity of news, the damp state of the decks, and the want of the morning papers, it was very charming indeed. Then the traveller got a little restive, and began to peer closely into the fog, and look aloft to see if he could make out the stay-sails, and then he entered into a long confidential talk with the captain, in relation to the chances of "getting on," of a fresh breeze springing up, and the fog lifting; whether we should make Louisburgh by to-morrow night, and if not, when; with various other salt-water speculations and problems. Then Picton climbed up on the patent-windlass to get a full view of the fog at the end of the bow-sprit, and took another survey of the buried stay-sails, and the flying-jib. Then he and the Newfoundland sailor on the look-out, had a long consultation of great gravity and importance; and finally he turned around and came up to the place where I was standing, and broke out: "I say, what the devil are we to do with ourselves this morning?"

"What are we to do?" That eternal question. It instantly seemed to double the thickness of the fog, to arrest the slow movement of the vessel. Picton had nothing to do for a fortnight, and I had left home with the sole object of going somewhere where soul and body could rest. "Nothing to do," was precisely the one thing needful. "Nothing to do," is exquisite happiness, for real happiness is but a negation. "Nothing to do," is repose for the body, respite for the mind. It is an ideal hammock swinging in drowsy tropical groves, apart from the roar of the busy, relentless world; away from the strife of faction, the toils of business, the restless stretch of ambition, wealth's tinsel pride, poverty's galling harness. "Nothing to do," is the phantom of young Imagination, the evanescent hope that promises to crown

"A youth of labor with an age of ease."

"Nothing to do," was the charm that lured us on board the "Balaklava," and now "nothing to do," was with us like the Bottle-Imp, an incubus, still crying out: "You may yet exchange me for a smaller coin, if such there be!" "Nothing to do," is an imposture. Something to do is the very life of life, the beginning and end of being. "Picton," said I, "one thing we must do, at least, this morning."

"What is that?" replied the traveller, eagerly opening his mackintosh, and drawing it off so as to be ready to do it.

"Taking into consideration the slow and sleepy nature of this climate, the thickness of the fog, the faint, thin air that impels the vessel, the early time of day, and the regulations of the 'Balaklava,' it seems to me we shall have to be steadily occupied, for at least three hours, in waiting for breakfast."

Then Picton got hungry! He was a large, stout man, wrapped up by a multitude of garments to the thickness of a polar bear, and when he got hungry, it was on a scale of corresponding dimensions. First he alluded to the fact that we had gone supperless to bed the night before; then he buttoned up his mackintosh, had a brief interview with the captain, shouted down the gang-way for the cook, and finally disappeared in the forecastle. Then he came up again with that officer, rummaged in the galley for the ship's hatchet, and split up all the kindling-wood on deck; then he shed his petals (mackintosh and over-coats) and instructed Cookey in the mystery of building a fire. Then he emerged from the intolerable smoke he had raised in the galley, and devoted himself to the stove-pipe outside, Cookey, meanwhile, within the caboose, getting the benefit of all the experiments.

At last a faint smell of coffee issued forth from the caboose, a little Arabia breathed through the humid atmosphere, and a sound, as if Cookey were stirring the berries in a pan, was heard in the midst of the smoke. Meanwhile Picton descends in the hold with a bucket of salt-water to enjoy the luxury of a bath, and reappears in full toilet just as Cookey is grinding the berries, burnt and green, with a hand-mill between his knees. The pan by this time is put to a new use; it is now lined with bacon in full frizzle; presently it will be turned to account as a bake-pan, for pearl-ash cakes of chrome-yellow complexion: everything must take its turn; the pan is the actor of all work; it accepts coffee, cakes, pork, fish, pudding, besides being general dish-washer and soup-warmer, as we found out before long.

During the preparation of these successive courses, Picton and I sat on deck in hungry silence. Now and then an anxious glance at the galley, or a tormenting whiff of the savory viands, would give new life to the demon that raged within us. I believe if Cookey had accidentally upset the coffee tea-kettle, and put out the fire, his sanctuary would have been sacked instantly. Eight o'clock came, and yet we had not broken bread. We walked up and down the deck to relieve our appetites. At last we saw the three cracked mugs, our tea-cups, which had been our ale-glasses of the night before, brought up for a rinse, and then we knew that breakfast was not far off. The cloth was spread, the saffron cakes, ship's butter, yellow mugs, coffee, pork, and pismires temptingly arrayed. We did not wait to hear the cook ring the bell. We watched him ashe came up with it in his hand, and squeezed past him before he shook out a single vibration.

Then we made a Meal!

Breakfast being over, the fog lightened a little. Our tiny horizon widened its boundaries a few hundred feet, or so; we could see once more the top-mast of the schooner. So we lazily swung along, with nothing to do again. Sometimes a distant fog-bell; sometimes a distant sound across the face of the deep, like the falling of cataract waters.

"What is that sound, Bruce?"

"It's the surf breakin' on the rocks," responds Bruce; "I hae been listenen to it for hoors."

"Are we then so near shore?"

"About three miles aff," replies the mate.

Presently we heard the sound of human voices; a laugh; the stroke of oars in the row-locks, plainly distinguishable in the mysterious vapor. The captain hailed: "Hallo!" "Halloo!" echoes in answer. The strokes of the oars are louder and quicker; they are approaching us, but where? "Halloo!" comes again out of the mist. And again the captain shouts in reply. Then a white phantom boat, thin, vapory, unsubstantial, now seen, now lost again, appears on the skirts of our horizon.

"Where are we?" asks the captain.

"Off St. Esprit," answer the boatmen.

"What are you after?" asks the captain.

"Looking for our nets," is the reply; and once more boat and boatmen disappear in the luminous vapor. These are *mackerel fishermen*; their nets are adrift from their stone-anchors: the fish are used for bait in the cod-fisheries, as well as for salting down. If we could but come across the nets, what a rare treat we might have at dinner!

Lazily on we glide—nothing to do. Picton is reading a stunning book; the captain, his lady, the baby, and I making a small family circle around the wheel; the mate is on the look-out over the bows; all at once, he shouts out: "*There they are! the nets!*" Down goes Picton's book on the deck; Bruce catches up a rope and fastens it to a large iron hook; the sailors run to the side of the vessel; captain releases his forefinger from baby's hand, and catches the wheel; all is excitement in a moment. "*Starboard!*" shouts the mate, as the nets come sweeping on, directly in front of the cut-water. The schooner obeys the wheel, sheers off, and now, as the floats come along sidewise, Bruce has dropped his hook in the mesh—*it takes hold!* and the heavy mass is partially raised up in the water. "Thousands of them," says Picton; sure enough, the whole net is alive with mackerel, splashing, quivering, glistening. "Catch hold here, I canna hold them; O the beauties!" says the mate. Some grasp at the rope, others look around for another hook. "Hauld 'em! hauld 'em!" shouts Bruce; but the weighty piscatorial mass is too much for us, it will drag us desperately along the deck to the stern of the vessel. The schooner is going slowly, but still she is going. Another hook is rigged and thrown at the struggling mesh; but it breaks loose, the mackerel are dragging behind the rudder; we are at our rope's end. At last, rope, hook, and nets are abandoned, and again we have nothing to do.

High noon, and a red spot visible overhead; the captain brings out his sextant to take an observation. This proceeding we viewed with no little interest, and, for the humor of the thing, I borrowed the sextant of the captain and took a satirical view of a great luminary in obscurity. As I had the instrument upside down, the sailors were in convulsions of laughter; but why should we not make everybody happy when we have it in our power?

High noon, and again hunger overtook us. Picton, by this time, had brought out the cans of preserved meats, the curried tin chicken, the portable soup, the ale and pickles. The cook was put upon duty; pot and pan were scoured for more delicate viands; Picton was *chef de cuisine*; we had a magnificent banquet that day on the "Balaklava."

To give a zest to the entertainment, the captain's lady dined with us; the mate kindly undertaking the charge of the baby.

When we came on deck, after a repast that would have been perfect but for the absence of potatoes, Bruce was marching up and down, dangling the baby in a way that made it appear all legs; "I doan't see," said he, "hoo a wummun can lug a baby all day aboot in her airms! I hae only carried this one half an 'our, and boath airms is sore. But I suppose it's naturely, it's naturely—everything to its nature."

The dinner having been a success, Picton was in great spirits for the rest of the day. The fog spread its munificent halo around us, and before nightfall broke into myriads of white rainbows—sea-dogs the sailors call them—and finally lifted so high that we could see the spectral moon shining through the thin rack. Once more we sang "Annie Laurie;" the traveller brought out his travelling blanket for a dewy slumber on deck; the lady of the

"Balaklava" put on her night-cap and retired with baby to the double berth: Bruce took the helm. As I was passing the light in the binnacle, I looked in at the compass for a moment. "She's nailed there," said the old mate. Nailed there, true to her course, as steadfast to the guiding rudder as truth is to religion. We were but a few miles from a dangerous coast, in a vessel of the frailest kind, but she was "nailed there," obedient to man's intelligence, and that was security and safety. What a text to say one's prayers upon!

"Picton," said I, the next morning, after the schooner-breakfast, "it seems to me the strangest thing that Mrs. Capstan should have the pure Irish pronunciation and the mate the thorough Scotch brogue, although both were born in Newfoundland, and of Newfoundland parents. I must confess to no small amount of surprise at the complete isolation of the people of these colonies; the divisions among them; the separate pursuits, prejudices, languages; they seem to have nothing in common; no aggregation of interests; it is existence without nationality; sectionalism without emulation; a mere exotic life with not a fibre rooted firmly in the soil. The colonists are English, Irish, Scotch, French, for generation after generation. Why is this, O Picton? Why is it that the captain's lady has high cheek-bones, and speaks the pure Hibernise? why is the only railroad in the colony but nine and three-quarter miles long, and the great Shubenacadie Canal yet unfinished, although it was begun in the year 1826; a canal fifty-three mortal miles in length, already engineered and laid out by nature in a chain of lakes, most conveniently arranged with the foot of each little lake at the head of the next one—like 'orient pearls at random strung'—requiring but a few locks to be complete: the head of the first lake lying only twelve hundred and ten yards from Halifax harbor, and the Shubenacadie River itself at the other end, emptying in the place of destination, namely, the Basin of Minas; a work that, if completed, would cut off more than three hundred miles of outside voyaging around a stormy, foggy, dangerous coast; a work that was estimated to cost but seventy-five thousand pounds, and for which fifteen thousand pounds had already been subscribed by the government; a work that would be the saving of so many vessels, crews, and cargoes of so much value; a work that would traverse one of the most fertile countries in America; a work that would bring the inland produce within a few hours of the seaboard; a work so necessary, so obvious, so easily completed, that no Yankee could see it undone, if it were within the limits of his county, and have one single night's rest until the waters were leaping from lock to lock, from lake to lake in one continuous flood of prosperity from Minas to Chebucto? Why is this, O traveller of the 'Balaklava?'"

"The reason of it all," replied Picton, with great equanimity of manner, "is entirely owing to the stupidity of the people here; the British government is the best government, sir, in the world; it fosters, protects, and supports the colonies, with a sort of parental care, sir; the colonies, sir, afford no recompense to the British government for its care and protection, sir; each colony is only a bill of expense, sir, to the mother country, and if, with all these advantages, the people of these colonies will persist, sir, in being behind the age, sir, what can we do to prevent it, I would like to know, sir?"

"It does seem to me, Picton, this fostering, protecting, and paying the governmental expenses of the colonies, is very like pampering and amusing a child with sweetmeats and nick-nacks, and at the same time keeping it in leading-strings. It is very certain that these colonists would not be the same people if their ancestors had been transplanted, a century or so ago, to our side of the Bay of Fundy; no, not even if they had pitched their tents at the 'jumping-off place,' as it is called—Eastport, for even there they would have produced a crop of pure Yankees, although grown from divers nations, religions, and tongues."

Here Picton turned up his lip, and smiled out of a little battery of sarcasm: "And you think," said he, after a pause, "that these colonists would no longer revel in those little prejudices and sectionalisms so dear to every American heart, if they were transplanted to your own favored coasts? Why, sir, there is more sectionalism in the country you would transport these people to, than in any one nation I ever heard of; every one of your States is a petty principality; it has its own separate interests; its own bigoted boundaries; its conventionalisms; its pet laws; and as for its prejudices, I will just ask you, as a candid man, not as a Yankee, but as a traveller like myself, a cosmopolite, if you please, what you think of the two great eternal States of Massachusetts and South Carolina, and whether prejudices and sectionalisms are to be fairly charged upon these colonies, and upon them only?"

"Picton, I will be frank with you. The States you name are looked upon as the great game-cocks of the Union, and we give them a tolerably large arena to fight their battles in. Either champion has flapped its wings and crowed its loudest, and drawn in its local backers, but the great States of my country are not these two. I feel at this moment an almost irrepressible desire to instance a single one as an example; but insomuch as nobody has ever flapped wing or crowed because of it, I will not be the first to break the silence. This much I will say, there are some States, and those the very greatest in the Union, that neither claim to be, nor make a merit of being *provincial*."

"But, even in your State, you have your stately prejudices," said Picton, with a marked emphasis upon the "stately."

"No, sir, we have no stately prejudices, at least among those entitled to have them, the native-born citizens; nor do I believe such prejudices exist in many of the States with us at home, sir."

"But as you admit there is a sectional barrier between your people," said Picton, "I do not see why our form of government is not as wise as your form of government."

"The difference, Picton, is simply this: your government is foreign, and almost unchangeable; ours is local, and mutable as the flux and reflux of the tide. As a consequence, sectionalism is active with us, and apathetic with you. Your colonists have nothing to care for, and we have everything to care for."

"Then," said Picton, "we can sleep while you struggle?"

"Yes, Picton, that is the question——

'Whether 'tis best to roam or rest. The land's lap, or the water's breast?'

We think it is best to choose the active instead of the stagnant; if a man cannot take part in the great mechanism of humanity, better to die than to sleep. And Picton, so far as this is concerned, so far as the general interests of humanity are concerned, your colonists are only *dead men*, while our "stately" men are individually responsible, not only to their own kind, but to all human kind, and herein each form of government tells its own story."

"I think you are rather severe upon poor Nova Scotia this morning," said Picton, drily.

"You mistake me, Picton; I do not intend to cast any reflections upon the people; I am only contrasting the effects produced by two different forms of government upon neighboring bodies of men that would have been alike had either a republican or monarchical rule obtained over both."

"Likely," said Picton, sententiously.

Meantime the schooner was lazily holding her course through the fog, which was now dense as ever. What an odd little bit of ocean this is to be on! "The sea, the sea, the open sea," all your own, with a diameter of perhaps forty yards. Picton, who is full of activity, begins to unroll the log line; the captain turns the glass, away goes the log. "Stop," "not three knots!" and then comes the question again: "What shall we do?—we are getting becalmed!"

"By Jove!" said Picton, slapping his thigh, "I have it—*cod-fish*!"

There are plenty of hooks on board the "Balaklava," and unfortunately only one cod-line; but what with the deep-sea lead-and-line, and a roll of blue cord, with a spike for a sinker, and the hooks, we are soon in the midst of excitement. Now we almost pray for a calm; the schooner *will* heave ahead, and leave the lines astern; but nevertheless, up come the fine fish, and plenty of them, too; the deck is all flop and glister with cod, haddock, pollock; and Cookey, with a short knife, is at work with the largest, preparing them for the banquet, according to the code Newfoundland. Certainly the art of "cooking a cod-fish" is not quite understood, except in this part of the world. The white flakes do not exhibit the true conchoidal fracture in such perfection elsewhere; nor break off in such delicious morsels, edged with delicate brown. "Another bottle of ale, please, and a granitic biscuit, and a pickle, by way of dessert."

Lazily along swings the "Balaklava." Picton brings up his travelling blanket, and we stretch out upon it on deck, basking in the warm, humid light, and leisurely puffing away at our segars, for we have nothing else to do. Towards evening it grows colder, very much colder; over-coats are in requisition; the captain says we are nearing some icebergs; the fog folds itself up and hangs above us in strips of cloud, or rolls away in voluminous masses to the edges of the horizon. The stars peep out between the strips overhead, the moon sends forth her silver vapors and finally emerges from the "crudded clouds;" the wake of the schooner is one long phosphoric trail of flame; the masts are creaking, sails stretching, the waters pouring against the bows; out on the deep, white crests lift and break, the winds are loosened, and now good speed to the "Balaklava." Meanwhile, the hitherto listless Newfoundland men are now wide awake, and busy; the man at the wheel is on the alert; the captain is looking at his charts; Picton and I walking the deck briskly, but unsteadily, to keep off the cold; Mrs. Capstan has turned in with the baby. Blacker and larger waves are rising, with whiter crests; on and on goes the schooner with dip and rise—tossing her yards as a stag tosses his antlers. On and on goes the brave "Balaklava," the captain at the bows on the look-out; the sky is mottled with clouds, but fortunately there is no fog; nine, ten o'clock, and at last a light begins to lift in the distance. "Is it Louisburgh light, captain?" "I don't make it out yet," replies Captain Capstan, "but I think it is not." After a pause, he adds: "Now I see what it is; it is Scattarie light—we have passed Louisburgh."

This was not pleasant; we had undertaken the voyage for the sake of visiting the old French town. To be sure, it was a great disappointment. But then we were rapidly nearing Scattarie light; and after we doubled the island, the wind would be right astern of us, and by breakfast time we would be in the harbor of Sydney.

"Captain," said we, after a brief consultation, "we will leave the matter entirely to you; although we had hoped to see Louisburgh this night, yet we can visit it overland to-morrow; and as the wind is so favorable for you, why, crack on to Sydney, if you like."

With that we resumed our walk to keep up the circulation.

"It is strange," said Picton, "the captain should have passed the light without seeing it."

"Ever since we left Richmond," said the man at the wheel, "his eyes has been weak, so as he couldn't see as good as common."

"Did you see the light?" we asked.

"Oh, yes; I can see it now, right astern of us."

We looked, and at last made it out: a faint, nebulous star, upon the very edge of the gloomy waters.

"There is the light, captain."

"Where?"

"Right astern."

The captain walked aft to the steersman and peered anxiously in the distance. Then he came forward again, and shouted down the forecastle: "Hallo, hallo, turn out there! all hands on deck! turn out, men! turn out!"

"What now, captain?"

"Nothing," said he, "only I am going to *about-ship*."

And sure enough, the little schooner came up to the wind; the men hauled away at the sheets, the sails fluttered—filled upon the new tack, and in a few minutes our bows were pointed for Louisburgh.

The "Balaklava" had barely broadened out her sails to the fair wind, after she had been put about, when we were conscious of an increased straining and chirping of the masts and sails, an uneasy, laborious motion of the vessel; of blacker and larger waves, of whiter and higher crests, that sometimes broke over the bows, even, and made the deck wet and slippery. The moon was now rising high, but the clouds were rapidly thickening, and her majesty seemed to be reeling from side to side, as we bore on, with plunge and shudder, for the light ahead of us. Bruce had taken the wheel; all hands were on deck, and all busy, hauling upon this rope or that, taking in the stay-sails and flying-jib, as the captain shouted out from time to time; and looking ahead, with no little appearance of anxiety.

"Ah! she's a pretty creature," said the mate; "look there," nodding with his head at the compass, "did'na I tell you? She's nailed there." Then he broke out again: "Ay, she's a flyin' noo; see hoo she's *raisin' the light*!"

It was, indeed, surprising to see the great beacon rising higher and higher out of the water.

"Is it a good harbor, Bruce?"

"*When ye get in*," answered the mate; "but it's narrar, it's narrar; ye can pitch a biscuit ashore as ye go through; and inside o't is the 'Nag's Head,' a sunken bit o' rock, with about five feet water; if ye miss that, ye're aw right!" We were now rapidly approaching the beacon, and could fairly see the rocks and beach in the track of its light. On the other side there were great masses of savage surf, whirling high up in the night, the indications of the three islands on the west of the harbor. The captain had climbed up in the rigging to keep a good look-out ahead; the light of the beacon broadened on the deck; we were within the very jaws of the crags and surf; the wild ocean beating against the doors of the harbor; the churning, whirling, whistling danger on either side, lighted up by the glare of the beacon! past we go, and, with a sweep, the "Balaklava" evades the "Nag's Head," and rounding too, drops sail and anchor beside the walls of Louisburgh.

Then the thick fog, which had been pursuing us, came, and enveloped all in obscurity.

"It is lucky," said Captain Capstan, "that it didn't come ten minutes sooner."

CHAPTER V.

Louisburgh—The Great French Fortress—Incidents of the Old French War—Relics of the Siege—Description of the Town—The two Expeditions—A Yankee *ruse de guerre*—The Rev. Samuel Moody's Grace—Wolfe's Landing—The Fisherman's Hutch—The Lost Coaster—The Fisheries—Picton tries his hand at a fish-pugh.

Nearly a century has elapsed since the fall of Louisburgh. The great American fortress of Louis XV. surrendered to Amherst, Wolfe, and Boscawen in 1758. A broken sea-wall of cut stone; a vast amphitheatre, inclosed within a succession of green mounds; a glacis; and some miles of surrounding ditch, yet remain—the relics of a structure for which the treasury of France paid Thirty Millions of Livres!

We enter where had been the great gate, and walk up what had been the great avenue. The vision follows undulating billows of green turf that indicate the buried walls of a once powerful military town. Fifteen thousand people were gathered in and about these walls; six thousand troops were locked within this fortress, when the key turned in the stupendous gate.

A hundred years since, the very air of the spot where we now stand, vibrated with the chime of the church-bells and the roll of the stately organ, or wafted to devout multitudes the savor of holy incense. Here were congregated the soldiers, merchants, artisans of old France; on these high walls paced the solemn sentry; in these streets the nun stole past in her modest hood; or the romantic damsel pressed her cheek to the latticed window, as the young officer rode by and, martial music filled the avenues with its inspiring strains; in yonder bay floated the great war-ships of Louis; and around the shores of this harbor could be counted battery after battery, with scores of guns bristling from the embrasures.

The building of this stronghold was a labor of twenty-five years. The stone walls rose to the height of thirty-six feet. In those broken arches, studded with stalactites, those casemates, or vaults of the citadel, you still see some evidence of its former strength. You will know the citadel by them, and by the greater height of the mounds which mark the walls that once encompassed it. Within these stood the smaller military chapel. Think of looking down from this point upon those broad avenues, busy with life, a hundred years ago!

Neither roof nor spire remain now; nor square nor street; nor convent, church, or barrack. The green turf covers all: even the foundations of the houses are buried. It is a city without an inhabitant. Dismantled cannon, with the rust clinging in great flakes; scattered implements of war; broken weapons, bayonets, gun-locks, shot, shell or grenade, unclaimed, untouched, corroded and corroding, in silence and desolation, with no signs of life visible within these once warlike parapets except the peaceful sheep, grazing upon the very brow of the citadel, are the only relics of once powerful Louisburgh.

Let us recall the outlines of its history. In the early part of the last century, just after the death of Louis XIV., these foundations were laid, and the town named in honor of the ruling monarch. Nova

Scotia proper had been ceded, by recent treaty, to the filibusters of Old and New-England, but the ancient Island of Cape Breton still owned allegiance to the lilies of France. Among the beautiful and commodious harbors that indent the southern coast of the island, this one was selected as being most easy of access. Although naturally well adapted for defence, yet its fortification cost the government immense sums of money, insomuch as all the materials for building had to be brought from a distance. Belknap thus describes it: "It was environed, two miles and a half in circumference, with a rampart of stone from thirty to thirty-six feet high, and a ditch eighty feet wide, with the exception of a space of two hundred yards near the sea, which was inclosed by a dyke and a line of pickets. The water in this place was shallow, and numerous reefs rendered it inaccessible to shipping, while it received an additional protection from the side-fire of the bastions. There were six-bastions and eight batteries, containing embrasures for one hundred and forty-eight cannon, of which forty-five only were mounted, and eight mortars. On an island at the entrance of the harbor was planted a battery of thirty cannon, carrying twenty-eight pound shot; and at the bottom of the harbor was a grand, or royal battery, of twenty-eight cannon, forty-two pounders, and two eighteen-pounders. On a high cliff, opposite to the island-battery, stood a light house, and within this point, at the north-east part of the harbor, was a careening wharf, secure from all winds, and a magazine of naval stores. The town was regularly laid out in squares; the streets were broad and commodious, and the houses, which were built partly of wood upon stone foundations, and partly of more durable materials, corresponded with the general appearance of the place. In the centre of one of the chief bastions was a stone building, with a moat on the side near the town, which was called the citadel, though it had neither artillery nor a structure suitable to receive any. Within this building were the apartments of the governor, the barracks for the soldiers, and the arsenal; and, under the platform of the redoubt, a magazine well furnished with military stores. The parish church, also, stood within the citadel, and without was another, belonging to the hospital of St. Jean de Dieu, which was an elegant and spacious structure. The entrance to the town was over a drawbridge, near which was a circular battery, mounting sixteen guns of fourteen-pound shot."

This cannon-studded harbor was the naval dépôt of France in America, the nucleus of its military power, the protector of its fisheries, the key of the gulf of St. Lawrence, the Sebastopol of the New World. For a quarter of a century it had been gathering strength by slow degrees: Acadia, poor inoffensive Acadia, from time to time, had been the prey of its rapacious neighbors; but Louisburgh had grown amid its protecting batteries, until Massachusetts felt that it was time for the armies of Gad to go forth and purge the threshing-floor with such ecclesiastical iron fans as they were wont to waft peace and good will with, wherever there was a fine opening for profit and edification.

The first expedition against Louisburgh was only justifiable upon the ground that the wants of New England for additional territory were pressing, and immediate action, under the circumstances, indispensable. Levies of colonial troops were made, both in and out of the territories of the saints. The forces, however, actually employed, came from Massachusetts, Connecticut, and

New Hampshire; the first supplying three thousand two hundred, the second five hundred, the third three hundred men. The coöperation of Commodore Warren, of the English West-Indian fleet, was solicited; but the Commodore declined, on the ground "that the expedition was wholly a provincial affair, undertaken without the assent, and probably without the knowledge, of the ministry." But Governor Shirley was not a man to stop at trifles. He had a heart of lignum vitæ, a rigid anti-papistical conscience, beetle brows, and an eye to the cod-fisheries. Higher authority than international law was pressed into the service. George Whitefield, then an itinerant preacher in New-England, furnished the necessary warrant for the expedition, by giving a motto for its banner: "*Nil desperandum Christo duce*"—Nothing is to be despaired of with Christ for leader. The command was, however, given to William Pepperel, a fish and shingle merchant of Maine. One of the chaplains of the filibusters carried a hatchet specially sharpened, to hew down the wooden images in the churches of Louisburgh. Everything that was needed to encourage and cheer the saints, was provided by Governor Shirley, especially a goodly store of New England rum, and the Rev. Samuel Moody, the lengthiest preacher in the colonies. Louisburgh, at that time feebly garrisoned, held out bravely in spite of the formidable array concentrated against it. In vain the Rev. Samuel Moody preached to its high stone walls; in vain the iconoclast chaplain brandished his ecclesiastical hatchet; in vain Whitefield's banner flaunted to the wind. The fortress held out against shot and shell, saint, flag and sermon. New England ingenuity finally circumvented Louisburgh. Humiliating as the confession is, it must be admitted that our pious forefathers did actually abandon "Christo duce," and used instead a little worldly artifice.

Commodore Warren, who had declined taking a part in the siege of Louisburgh, on account of the regulations of the service, had received, after the departure of the expedition, instructions to keep a look-out for the interests of his majesty in North America, which of course could be readily interpreted, by an experienced officer in his majesty's service, to mean precisely what was meant to be meant. As a consequence, Commodore Warren was speedily on the look-out, off the coast of Cape Breton, and in the course of events fell in with, and captured, the "Vigilant," seventy-four, commanded by Captain Stronghouse, or, as his title runs, "the Marquis de la Maison Forte." The "Vigilant" was a store-ship, filled with munitions of war for the French town. Here was a glorious opportunity. If the saints could only intimate to Duchambon, the Governor of Louisburgh, that his supplies had been cut off, Duchambon might think of capitulation. But unfortunately the French were prejudiced against the saints, and would not believe them under oath. But when probity fails, a little ingenuity and artifice will do quite as well. The chief of the expedition was equal to the emergency. He took the Marquis of Stronghouse to the different ships on the station, where the French prisoners were confined, and showed him that they were treated with great civility; then he represented to the Marquis that the New England prisoners were cruelly dealt with in the fortress of Louisburgh; and requested him to write a letter, in the name of humanity, to Duchambon, Governor, in behalf of those suffering saints; "expressing his approbation of the conduct of the English, and entreating similar usuage for those whom the fortune of war had thrown in his hands." The Marquis wrote the letter; thus it begins: "On board the 'Vigilant,' where I am a prisoner, before Louisburgh, June thirteen, 1745." The rest of the letter is unimportant. The confession of Captain Stronghouse, that he was a prisoner, was the point; and the consequences thereof, which had been foreseen by the filibustering besiegers, speedily followed. In three days Louisburgh capitulated.

Then the Rev. Samuel Moody greatly distinguished himself. He was a painful preacher; the most untiring, persevering, long-winded, clamorous, pertinacious vessel at craving a blessing, in the provinces. There was a great feast in honor of the occasion. But more formidable than the siege itself, was the anticipated "grace" of Brother Moody. New England held its breath when he began, and thus the Reverend Samuel: "Good Lord, we have so many things to thank Thee for, that time will be infinitely too short to do it; we must therefore leave it for the work of eternity."

Upon this there was great rejoicing, yea, more than there had been upon the capture of the French stronghold. Who shall say whether Brother Moody's brevity may not stretch farther across the intervals of time than the longest preaching ever preached by mortal preacher?

In three years after its capture, Louisburgh was restored to the French by the treaty of Aix-la-Chapelle. Ten years after its restoration, a heavier armament, a greater fleet, a more numerous army, besieged its almost impregnable walls. Under Amherst, Boscawen, and Wolfe, no less than twenty-three ships of war, eighteen frigates, sixteen thousand land forces, with a proportionable train of cannon and mortars, were arrayed against this great fortress in the year 1758. Here, too, many of our own ancestral warriors were gathered in that memorable conflict; here Gridley, who afterwards planned the redoubt at Bunker Hill, won his first laurels as an engineer; here Pomeroy distinguished himself, and others whose names are not recorded, but whose deeds survive in the history of a republic. The very drum that beat to arms before Louisburgh was braced again when the greater drama of the Revolution opened at Concord and Lexington.

The siege continued for nearly two months. From June 8th until July 26th, the storm of iron and fire—of rocket, shot, and shell—swept from yonder batteries, upon the castellated city. Then when the King's, the Queen's, the Dauphin's bastions were lying in ruins, the commander, Le Chevalier de Drucour, capitulated, and the lilies of the Bourbon waved over Louisburgh no more.

And here we stand nearly a century after, looking out from these war-works upon the desolate harbor. At the entrance, the wrecks of three French frigates, sunk to prevent the ingress of the British fleet, yet remain; sometimes visited by our still enterprising countrymen, who come down in coasters with diving-bell and windlass, to raise again from the deep, imbedded in sea-shells, the great guns that have slept in the ooze so long. Between those two points lay the ships of the line, and frigates of Louis; opposite, where the parapets of stone are yet visible, was the grand battery of forty guns: at Lighthouse Point yonder, two thousand grenadiers, under General Wolfe, drove back the French artillerymen, and tamed their cannon upon these mighty walls. Here the great seventy-four blew up; there the English boats were sunk by the guns of the fortress; day and night for many weeks this ground has shuddered with the thunders of the cannonade.

And what of all this? we may ask. What of the ships that were sunk, and those that floated away with the booty? What of the soldiers that fell by hundreds here, and those that lived? What of the prisoners that mourned, and the captors that triumphed? What of the flash of artillery, and the shattered wall that answered it? Has any benefit resulted to mankind from this brilliant achievement? Can any man, of any nation, stand here and say: "This work was wrought to my profit?" Can any man draw such a breath here amid these buried walls, as he can upon the humblest sod that ever was wet with the blood of patriotism? I trow not.

A second time in possession of this stronghold, England had not the means to maintain her conquest; the fortification was too large for any but a powerful garrison. A hundred war-ships had congregated in that harbor: frigates, seventy-fours, transports, sloops, under the *Fleur-de-lis*. Although Louisburgh was the pivot-point of the French possessions, yet it was but an outside harbor for the colonies. So the order went forth to destroy the town that had been reared with so much cost, and captured with so much sacrifice. And it took two solid years of gunpowder to blow up these immense walls, upon which we now sadly stand, O gentle reader! Turf, turf, turf covers all! The gloomiest spectacle the sight of man can dwell upon is the desolate, but once populous, abode of humanity. Egypt itself is cheerful compared with Louisburgh!

"It rains," said Picton.

It had rained all the morning; but what did that matter when a hundred years since was in one's mind? Picton, in his mackintosh, was an impervious representative of the nineteenth century; but I was as fully saturated with water as if I were living in the place under the old French *régime*.

"Let us go down," said Picton, "and see the jolly old fishermen outside the walls. What is the use of staying here in the rain after you have seen all that can be seen? Come along. Just think how serene it will be if we can get some milk and potatoes down there."

There are about a dozen fishermen's huts on the beach outside the walls of the old town of Louisburgh. When you enter one it reminds you of the descriptive play-bill of the melo-drama— "Scene II.: Interior of a Fisherman's Cottage on the Sea-shore: Ocean in the Distance." The walls are built of heavy timbers, laid one upon another, and caulked with moss or oakum. Overhead are square beams, with pegs for nets, poles, guns, boots, the heterogeneous and picturesque tackle with which such ceilings are usually ornamented. But oh! how clean everything is! The knots are fairly scrubbed out of the floor-planks, the hearth-bricks red as cherries, the dresser-shelves worn thin with soap and sand, and white as the sand with which they have been scoured. I never saw drawing-room that could compare with the purity of that interior. It was cleanliness itself; but I saw many such before I left Louisburgh, in both the old town and the new.

We sat down in the "hutch," as they call it, before a cheery wood-fire, and soon forgot all about the outside rain. But if we had shut out the rain, we had not shut out the neighboring Atlantic. That was near enough; the thunderous surf, whirling, pouring, breaking against the rocky shore and islands, was sounding in our ears, and we could see the great white masses of foam lifted against the sky from the window of the hutch, as we sat before the warm fire.

"You was lucky to get in last night," said the master of the hutch, an old, weather-beaten fisherman.

"Yes," replied Picton, surveying the grey head before him with as much complacency as he would a turnip; "and a serene old place it is when we get in."

To this the weather-beaten replied by winking twice with both eyes.

"Rather a dangerous coast," continued Picton, stretching out one thigh before the fire. "I say, don't you fishermen often lose your lives out there?" and he pointed to the mouth of the harbor.

"There was only two lives lost *in seventy years*," replied the old man (this remarkable fact was confirmed by many persons of whom we asked the same question during our visit), "and one of them was a young man, a stranger here, who was capsized in a boat as he was going out to a vessel in the harbor."

"You are speaking now of lives lost in the fisheries," said Picton, "not in the coasting trade."

"Oh!" replied the old man, shaking his head, "the coasting trade is different; there is a many lives lost in that. Last year I had a brother as sailed out of this in a shallop, on the same day as yon vessel," pointing to the Balaklava; "he went out in company with your captain; he was going to his wedding, he thought, poor fellow, for he was to bring a young wife home with him from Halifax, but he got caught in a storm off Canseau, and we never heard of the shallop again. He was my youngest brother, gentlemen."

It was strange to be seated in that old cottage, listening to so dreary a story, and watching the storm outside. There was a wonderful fascination in it, nevertheless, and I was not a little loth to leave the bright hearth when the sailors from the schooner came for us and carried us on board again to dinner.

The storm continued; but Picton and I found plenty to do that day. Equipped with oil-skin pea-jackets and sou'-westers, with a couple of *fish-pughs*, or poles, pointed with iron, we started on a cruise after lobsters, in a sort of flat-bottomed skiff, peculiar to the place, called a *dingledekooch*. And although we did not catch one lobster, yet we did not lose sight of many interesting particulars that were scattered around the harbor. And first of the fisheries. All the people here are directly or indirectly engaged in this business, and to this they devote themselves entirely; farming being scarcely thought of. I doubt whether there is a plough in the place; certainly there was not a horse, in either the old or new town, or a vehicle of any kind, as we found out betimes.

The fishing here, as in all other places along the coast, is carried on in small, clinker-built boats, sharp at both ends, and carrying two sails. It is marvellous with what dexterity these boats are handled; they are out in all weathers, and at all times, night or day, as it happens, and although sometimes loaded to the gunwale with fish, yet they encounter the roughest gales, and ride out storms in safety, that would be perilous to the largest vessels.

"I can carry all sail," said one old fellow, "when the captain there would have to take in every rag on the schooner."

And such, too, was the fact. These boats usually sail a few miles from the shore, rarely beyond twelve; the fish are taken with hand-lines generally, but sometimes a set line with buoys and anchors is used. The fish, are cured on *flakes*, or high platforms, raised upon poles from the beach, so that one end of the staging is over the water. The cod are thrown up from the boat to the flake by means of the fish-pugh—a sort of one-pronged, piscatory pitchfork—and cleaned, salted, and cured there; then spread out to dry on the flake, or on the beach, and packed for market. *Nothing can be neater and cleaner than the whole system of curing the fish!* popular opinion to the contrary notwithstanding. The fishermen of Louisburgh are a happy, contented, kind, and simple people. Living, as they do, far from the jarring interests of the busy world, having a common revenue, for the ocean supplies each and all alike; pursuing an occupation which is constant discipline for body and soul; brave, sincere, and hospitable by nature, for all of these virtues are inseparable from their relations to each other; one can scarcely be with them, no matter how brief the visit, without feeling a kindred sympathy; without having a vague thought of "sometime I may be only too glad to escape from the world and accept this humble happiness instead;" without a dreamy idea of "Perhaps *this*, after all, is the real Arcadia!"

While I was indulging in these reflections, it was amusing to see Picton at work! The heads and entrails of the cod-fish, thrown from the "flakes" into the water, attract thousands of the baser tribes, such as sculpins, flounders, and toad-fish, who feed themselves fat upon the offals, and enjoy a peaceful life under the clear waters of the harbor. As the dingledekooch floated silently over them, they lay perfectly quiet and unsuspicious of danger, although within a few feet of the fatal fish-pugh, and in an element almost as transparent as air. Lobster, during the storm, had gone off to other grounds; but here were great flat flounders and sculpin, within reach of the indefatigable Picton. Down went the fish-pugh and up came the game! The bottom of the skiff was soon covered with the spearings of the traveller. Great flounders, those sub-marine buckwheat cakes; sculpins, bloated with rage and wind, like patriots out of office; toad-fish, savage and vindictive as Irishmen in a riot. Down went the fish-pugh! It was rare sport, and no person could have enjoyed it more than Picton—except perhaps some of the veteran fishermen of Louisburgh, who were gathered on the beach watching the doings in the dingledekooch.

CHAPTER VI.

A most acceptable Invitation—- An Evening in the Hutch—Old Songs—Picton in High Feather—Wolfe and Montcalm—Reminiscences of the Siege—Anecdotes of Wolfe—A Touch of Rhetoric and its Consequences.

Quite a little crowd of fishermen gathered around us, as the dingledekooch ran bows on the beach, and Picton, warm with exercise and excitement, leaped ashore, flourishing his piscatorial javelin with an air of triumph, which oddly contrasted with the faces of the Louisburghers, who looked at him and at his game, with countenances of great gravity—either real or assumed. Presently, another boat ran bows on the beach beside our own, and from this jumped Bruce, our jolly first mate, who had come ashore to spend a few hours with an old friend, at one of the hutches. To this we were hospitably invited also, and were right glad to uncase our limbs of stiff oil-skin and doff our sou'-westers, and sit down before the cheery fire, piled up with spruce logs and hackmatack; comfortable, indeed, was it to be thus snugly housed, while the weather outside was so lowering, and the schooner wet and cold with rain. To be sure, our gay and festive hall was not so brilliant as some, but it was none the less acceptable on that account; and, before long, a fragrant rasher of bacon, fresh eggs, white bread, and a strong cup of bitter tea made us feel entirely happy. Then these viands being removed, there came pipes and tobacco; and as something else was needed to crown the symposium, Picton whispered a word in the ear of Bruce, who presently disappeared, to return again after a brief absence, with some of our stores from the schooner. Then the table was decked again, with china mugs of dazzling whiteness, lemons, hot water, and a bottle of old Glenlivet; and from the centre of this gallant show, the one great lamp of the hutch cast its mellow radiance around, and nursed in the midst of its flame a great ball of red coal that burned like a bonfire. Then, when our host, the old fisherman, brought out a bundle of warm furs, of moose and cariboo skins, and distributed them around on the settles and broad, high-backed benches, so that we could loll at our ease, we began to realize a sense of being quite snug and cozy, and, indeed, got used to it in a surprisingly short space of time.

"Now, then," said Picton, "this is what I call serene," and the traveller relapsed into his usual activity; after a brief respite—"I say, give us a song, will you, now, some of you; something about this jolly old place, now—'Brave Wolfe,' or 'Boscawen,'" and he broke out—

"'My name d'ye see's Tom Tough, I've seen a little sarvice,Where mighty billows roll and loud tempests blow;I've sailed with noble Howe, and I've sailed with noble Jarvis,And in Admiral Duncan's fleet I've sung yeo, heave, yeo!And more ye must be knowin',I was cox'son to BoscawenWhen our fleet attacked Louisburgh,And laid her bulwarks low.But push about the grog, boys!Hang care, it killed a cat,Push about the grog, and sing—Yeo, heave, yeo!'"

"Good Lord!" said the old fisherman, "I harn't heard that song for more'n thirty years. Sing us another bit of it, please."

But Picton had not another bit of it; so he called lustily for some one else to sing. "Hang it, sing something," said the traveller.

"How stands the glass around;' that, you know, was written by Wolfe; at least, it was sung by him the night before the battle of Quebec, and they call it Wolfe's death song—

'How stands the glass around?For shame, ye take no care, my boys!How stands the glass around?'"

Here Picton forgot the next line, and substituted a drink for it, in correct time with the music:

"The trumpets sound;The colors flying are, my boys,To fight, kill, or wound'"——

Another slip of the memory [drink]:

"May we still be found,"

He has found it, and repeats emphatically:

"May we still be found!Content with our hard fare, my boys,

[all drink]

On the cold ground!'

"Then there is another song," said Picton, lighting his pipe with coal and tongs; "'Wolfe and Montcalm'—you must know that," he continued, addressing the old fisherman. But the ancient trilobite did not know it; indeed, he was not a singer, so Picton trolled lustily forth—

"'He lifted up his head,While the cannons did rattle,To his aid de camp he said,'How goes the battail?'The aid de camp, he cried,"'Tis in our favor;"Oh! then,' brave Wolfe replied,'I die with pleasure!'"

"There," said Picton, throwing himself back upon the warm and cosy furs, "I am at the end of my rope, gentlemen. Sing away, some of you," and the traveller drew a long spiral of smoke through his tube, and ejected it in a succession of beautiful rings at the beams overhead.

"Picton," said I, "what a strange, romantic interest attaches itself to the memory of Wolfe. The very song you have sung, 'How stands the glass around,' although not written by him, for it was composed before he was born, yet has a currency from the popular belief that he sang it on the evening preceding his last battle. And, indeed, it is by no means certain that Gray's Elegy does not derive additional interest from a kindred tradition."

"What is that?" said the traveller.

"Of course you will remember it. When Gray had completed the Elegy, he sent a copy of it to his friend, General Wolfe, in America; and the story goes, that as the great hero was sitting, wrapped in his military cloak, on board the barge which the sailors were rowing up the St. Lawrence, towards Quebec, he produced the poem, and read it in silence by the waning light of approaching evening, until he came to these lines, which he repeated aloud to his officers:

'The boast of heraldry, the pomp of power,And all that beauty, all that wealth e'er gave,Await alike the inevitable hour'——"

Then pausing for a moment, he finished the stanza:

"'The paths of glory lead but to the grave.'"

"Gentlemen," he added, "I would rather be the writer of this poem, than the greatest conqueror the world ever produced."

"That's true," said the old fisherman, sententiously. "We are all bound to that place, sometime or other."

"What place?" said Picton, rousing up.

"The berrying-ground," answered the ancient; "that is if we don't get overboard instead."

"But," he continued, "since you are speaking of General Wolfe, you must know my grandfather served under him at Minden, and at the battle here, too, where he was wounded, and left behind, when the general went back to England."

"I thought he went from this place to Quebec," said Picton.

"No, sir," replied the old man, "he went first to London, and came back again, and then went to Canada. Well," he continued, "my grandfather served under him, and was left here to get over his wownds, and so he married my grandmother, and lived in Louisburgh after the French were all sent away." Here the veteran placed his paws on the table, and looked out into the infinite. We could see we were in for a long story. "All the French soldiers and sailors, you see, were sent to England prisoners of war—and the rest of the people were sent to France; the governor of this here place was named Drucour; he was taken to Southampton, and put in prison. Well now, as I was saying, this hutch of mine was built by my father, just here by Wolfe's landing, for grandfather took a fancy to have it built on this spot; you see, Wolfe rowed over one night in a boat all alone from Lighthouse point yonder, and stood on the beach right under this here old wall, looking straight up at the French sentry over his head, and taking a general look at the town on both sides. There wasn't a man in all his soldiers who would have stood there at that time for a thousand pounds."

"What do you suppose the old file was doing over here?" inquired Picton, who was getting sleepy.

"I don't know," answered our host, "except it was his daring. He was the bravest man of his time, I've heard say—and so young"——

"Two and thretty only," said Bruce.

"And a tall, elegant officer, too," continued the ancient fisherman. "I've heard tell how the French governor's lady used to send him sweetmeats with a flag of truce, and he used to return his compliments and a pine apple, or something of that kind. Ah, he was a great favorite with the ladies! I've heard say, he was much admired for his elegant style of dancing, and always ambitious to have a tall and graceful lady for his partner, and then he was as much pleased as if he was in the thick of the fight. He was a great favorite with the soldiers, too; very careful of them, to see they were well nursed when they were sick, and sharing the worst and the best with them; but my grandfather used to say, very strict, too."

"Who was in command here, Wolfe or Amherst?"

"General Amherst was in command, and got the credit of it, too; but Wolfe did the fighting—so grandfather used to say."

"What was the name of his leddy in the old country?" said Bruce.

"I do not remember," replied the ancient, "but I've heard it. You know he was to be married, when he got back to England. And when the first shot struck him in the wrist, at Quebec, he took out her handkerchief from his breast-pocket, smiled, wrapped it about the place, and went on with the battle as if nothing had happened. But, soon after he got another wound, and yet he wasn't disheartened, but waved his ratan over his head, for none of the officers carried swords there, and kept on, until the third bullet went through and through his breast, when he fell back, and just breathed like, till word was brought that the French were retreating, when he said, then 'I am content,' and so closed his eyes and died."

Here there was a pause. Our entertainer, waving his hand towards our mugs of Glenlivet, by way of invitation, lifted his own to his mouth by the handle, and with a dexterous tilt that showed practice, turned its bottom towards the beams of the hutch.

"Do you remember any farther particulars of the siege of Louisburgh?" I asked.

"Oh, yes," replied the old man, "I remember grandfather telling us how he saw the bodies of fifteen or sixteen deserters hanging over the walls; they were Germans that had been sold to the French, four years before the war, by a Prussian colonel. Some of them got away, and came over to our side. He used to say, the old town looked like a big ship when they came up to it; it had two tiers of guns, one above the other, on the south—that is towards Gabarus bay, where our troops landed. And now I mind me of his telling that when they landed at Gabarus, they had a hard fight with the French and Indians, until Col. Fraser's regiment of Highlanders jumped overboard, and swam to a point on the rocks, and drove the enemy away with their broad-swords."

"That was the 63d Highlanders," said Bruce, with immense gravity.

"Among the Indians killed at Gabarus," continued our host, "they say there was one Micmac chief, who was six feet nine inches high. The French soldiers were very much frightened when the Highland men climbed up on the rocks; they called them English savages."

"That showed," said Bruce, "what a dommed ignorant set they were!"

"And, while I think of it," added our host, rising from his seat, "I have a bit of the old time to show you," and so saying, he retreated from the table, and presently brought forth a curious oak box from a mysterious corner of the hutch, and after some difficulty in drawing out the sliding cover, produced a roll of tawny newspapers, tied up with rope yarn, a colored wood engraving in a black frame—a portrait, with the inscription, "James Wolfe, Esq'r, Commander in Chief of His Majesty's Forces in the Expedition to Quebec," and on the reverse the following scrap from the London Chronicle of October 7, 1759:

"Amidst her conquests let Britannia groanFor Wolfe! her gallant, her undaunted son;For Wolfe, whose breast bright Honor did inspireWith patriot ardor and heroic fire;For Wolfe, who headed that intrepid band,Who, greatly daring, forced Cape Breton's strand.For Wolfe, who following still where glory call'd,No dangers daunted, no distress appall'd;Whose eager zeal disasters could not check,Intent to strike the blow which gained Quebec.For Wolfe, who, like the gallant Theban, dy'dIn th' arms of victory—his country's pride."

This inscription I read aloud, and then, under the influence of the loquacious potable, leaned back in my furry throne, crossed my hands over my forehead, looked steadily into the blazing fire-place, and continued the theme I had commenced an hour before.

"What a strange interest attaches itself to the memory of Wolfe! A youthful hero, who, under less happy auspices, might have been known only as the competent drill-master of regiments, elevated by the sagacity of England's wisest statesman to a prominent position of command; there to exhibit his generalship; there to retrieve the long list of disasters which followed Braddock's defeat; there to annihilate forever every vestige of French dominion in the Americas; to fulfill gloriously each point of his mission; to achieve, not by long delays, but by rapid movements, the conquest of two of the greatest fortresses in the possession of the rival crown; to pass from the world amid the shouts of victory— content in the fullness of his fame, without outliving it! His was a noble, generous nature; brave without cruelty; ardent and warlike, yet not insensible to the tenderest impulses of humanity. To die betrothed and beloved, yet wedded only to immortal honor;

to leave a mother, with a nation weeping at her feet; to serve his country, without having his patriotism contaminated by titles, crosses, and ribbons; this was the most fortunate fate of England's greatest commander in the colonies! No wonder, then, that with a grateful sympathy the laurels of his mother country were woven with the cypress of her chivalric son; that hundreds of pens were inspired to pay some tribute to his memory; that every branch of representative art, from stone to ink, essayed to portray his living likeness; that parliament and pulpit, with words of eloquence and gratitude, uttered the universal sentiment!

"Brave Wolfe," I continued, "whose memory is linked with his no less youthful rival, Montcalm"——here I was interrupted by the voice of the mate of the Balaklava—

"I'll be dommed," said he, "if some person isn't afire!"

Then I unclasped my hands, opened my eyes, and looked around me.

The scene was a striking one. Right before me, with his grey head on the table, buried in his piscatorial paws, lay the master of the hutch, fast asleep. On a settle, one of the fishermen, who had been a devout listener to all the legends of the grandson of the veteran of Louisburgh, was in a similar condition; Bruce, our jolly first mate, with the pertinacity of his race, was wide awake, to be sure, but there were unmistakable signs of drowsiness in the droop of his eyelids; and Picton? That gentleman, buried in moose and cariboo skins, prostrate on a broad bench, drawn up close by the fire-place, was dreaming, probably, of sculpins, flounders, fish-pugh, and dingledekooch!

"I say! wake up here!" said the jolly mate of the Balaklava; bringing his fist down upon the table with an emphatic blow, that roused all the sleepers except the traveller. "I say, wake up!" reiterated Brace, shaking Picton by the shoulder. Then Picton raised himself from his couch, and yawned twice; walked to the table, seated himself on a bench, thrust his fingers through his black hair, and instantly fell asleep again, after shakin out into the close atmosphere of the hutch a stifling odor of animal charcoal.

"A little straw makes a great reek," said Bruce, laughing, "and when a mon gives out before his pipe, he is like to be burnet," and he pointed to a long black and brown singe on the worsted comforter of the traveller, by which we understood that Picton had fallen asleep, pipe in mouth, and then dropped his lighted *dudeen* just on the safest part of his neck.

Once again we roused the sleeper; and so, shaking hands with our hospitable host, we left the comfortable hutch at Wolfe's Landing, and were soon on our way to the jolly little schooner.

CHAPTER VII.

The other side of the Harbor—A Foraging Party—
Disappointment—Twilight at Louisburgh—Long Days and Early
Mornings—A Visit and View of an Interior—A Shark Story—
Picton inquires about a Measure—Hospitality and the Two Brave
Boys—Proposals for a Trip overland to Sydney.

To make use of a quaint but expressive phrase, "it is patent
enough," that travellers are likely to consume more time in
reaching a place than they are apt to bestow upon it when found.
And, I am ashamed to say, that even Louisburgh was not an
exception to this general truth; although perhaps certain reasons
might be offered in extenuation for our somewhat speedy departure
from the precincts of the old town. First, then, the uncertainty of a
sailing vessel, for the "Balaklava" was coquettishly courting any
and every wind that could carry her out of our harbor of refuge.
Next, the desire of seeing more of the surroundings of the ancient
fortress—the batteries on the opposite side, the new town, the
lighthouse, and the wild picturesque coast. Add to these the wish of
our captain to shift his anchorage, to get on the side where he
would have a better opening towards the ocean, "when the wind
came on to blow,"—to say nothing of being in the neighborhood of
his old friends, whose cottages dotted the green hill-sides across
the bay, as you looked over the bows of the jolly little schooner.
And there might have been other inducements—such as the hope of
getting a few pounds of white sugar, a pitcher of milk (delicious,
lacteous fluid, for which we had yearned so often amid the briny
waves); and last, but not least, a hamper of blue-nosed potatoes.
So, when the shades of the second evening were gathering

grandly and gloomily around the dismantled parapets, and Louisburgh lay in all the lovely and romantic light of a red and stormy sunset, it seemed but fitting that the cable-chain of the anchor should clank to the windlass, and the die-away song of the mariner should resound above the calm waters, and the canvas stretch towards the land opposite, that seemed so tempting and delectable. And presently the "Balaklava" bore away across the red and purple harbor for the new town, leaving in her wake the ruined walls of Louisburgh that rose up higher the further we sailed from them.

The schooner dropped anchor inside the little cove on the opposite side of the old town, which the reader will see by referring to the map; and the old battles of the years '45 and '58 were presently forgotten in the new aspects that were presented. The anchor was scarcely dropped fairly, before the yawl-boat was under the stroke of the oars, and Picton and I *en route* for the store-house; the general, particular, and only exchange in the whole district of Louisburgh. It was a small wooden building with a fair array of tarpaulin hats, oil-skin garments, shelves of dry-goods and crockery, and boxes and barrels, such as are usually kept by country traders: on the beach before it were the customary flake for drying fish, the brown winged boats, and other implements of the fisheries.

But alas! the new town, that looked so pastoral and pleasant, with its tender slopes of verdure, was not, after all, a Canaan, flowing with milk and blue-nosed potatoes. Neither was there white sugar, nor coffee, nor good black tea there; the cabin of the schooner being as well furnished with these articles of comfort as the store-house of McAlpin, towards which we had looked with such longing eyes. Indeed, I would not have cared so much about the disappointment myself, but I secretly felt sorry for Picton, who went rummaging about the barrels in search of something to eat or to drink. "No white sugar?" said the traveller. "*We don't have whitesugar in this town*," was the answer. "Nor coffee?" "No, Sir." And the tea had the same flavor of musty hay, with which we were so well acquainted. At last Picton stumbled over a prize—a bushel-basket half-filled with potatoes, whereat he raised a bugle-note of triumph.

It may seem strange that a gentleman of fine education, a traveller, who had visited the famous European capitals, London, Paris, Rome, Madrid, Vienna; who had passed between the Pillars of Hercules, and voyaged upon the blue Mediterranean, far as the Greek Archipelago; who had wandered through the galleries of the Vatican, and mused within the courts of the Alhambra; who had seen the fire-works on the carnival dome of St. Peter's, and the water-works of Versailles; the temples of Athens, and the Boboli gardens of Florence; the sculptures of Praxiteles, and the frescoes of Raphael; should exhibit such emotion as Picton exhibited, over a bushel-basket only half-filled with small-sized blue-nosed tubers. But Picton was only a man, and "*Homo sum——*" the rest of the sentence it is needless to quote. I saw at a glance that the potatoes were cut in halves for planting; but Picton was filled with the divine idea of a feast.

"I say, we want a peck of potatoes."

"A peck?" was the answer. "Why, man, I wouldn't sell ye my seed-potatoes at a guinea apiece."

Here was a sudden let-down; a string of the human violin snapped, just as it was keyed up to tuning point. Slowly and sorrowfully we regained the yawl after that brief and bitter experience, and a few strokes of the oars carried us to the side of the "Balaklava."

It may seem absurd and trifling to dwell upon such slight particulars in this itinerary of a month among the Blue Noses (as our brothers of Nova Scotia are called); but to give a correct idea of this rarely-visited part of the world, one must notice the salient points that present themselves in the course of the survey. Louisburgh would speedly become rich from its fisheries, if there were sufficient capital invested there and properly used. Halifax is now the only point of contact between it and the outside world; Halifax supplies it with all the necessary articles of life, and Halifax buys all the produce of its fisheries. Therefore, Halifax reaps all the profits on either side, both of buying and selling, in all not amounting to much—as the matter now stands. But insomuch as the sluggish blood of the colonies will never move without some quickening impulse from exterior sources, and as Louisburgh is only ten days' sail, under canvas, from New York, and as the fisheries there would rapidly grow by kindly nurture into importance, it does seem as if a moderate amount of capital diverted in that direction, would be a fortunate investment, both for the investor and hardy fishermen of the old French town.

I have alluded before to the long Acadian twilights, the tender and loving leave-takings between the day and his earth; just as two fond and foolish young people separate sometimes, or as the quaint old poet in Britannia's Pastorals describes it:

"Look as a lover, with a lingering kiss, About to part with the best half that's his: Fain would he stay, but that he fears to do it, And curseth time for so fast hastening to it: Now takes his leave, and yet begins anewTo make less vows than are esteemed true: Then says, he must be gone, and then doth findSomething he should have spoke that's out of mind: And while he stands to look for't in her eyes, Their sad, sweet glance so ties his facultiesTo think from what he parts that he is nowAs far from leaving her, or knowing how, As when he came; begins his former strain, To kiss, to vow, and take his leave again; Then turns, comes back, sighs, pants, and yet doth go, Fain to retire, and loth to leave her so."

Even so these fond and foolish old institutions part company in northern regions, and, at the early hour of two o'clock in the morning, the amorous twilight reappears in his foggy mantle, to look at the fair face of his ancient sweetheart in the month of June.

Tea being over, the "cluck" of the row-locks woke the echoes of the twilight bay, as our little yawl put off again for the new town, with a gay evening party, consisting of the captain, his lady, the baby, Picton and myself, with a brace of Newfoundland oarsmen. If our galley was not a stately one, it was at least a cheerful vessel, and as the keel grated on the snow-white pebbles of the beach, Picton and I sprang ashore, with all the gallantry of a couple of Sir Walter Raleighs, to assist the queen of the "Balaklava" upon *terra firma*. Her majesty being landed, we made a royal procession to the largest hutch on the green slope before us, the captain carrying the insignia of his marital office (the baby) with great pomp and awkward ceremony, in front, while his lady, Picton and I, loitered in the rear. We had barely crossed the sill of the hutch-door, before we felt quite at home and welcome. The same cheery fire in the chimney-place, the spotless floor, the tidy rush-bottomed chairs, and a whole nest of little white-heads and twinkling eyes, just on the border of a bright patchwork quilt, was invitation enough, even if we had not been met at the threshold by the master himself, who stretched out his great arms with a kind, "Come-in-and-how-are-ye-all."

And what a wonderful evening we passed in that other hutch, before the blazing hearth-fire! What stories of wrecks and rescues, of icebergs and whales, of fogs and fisheries, of domestic lobsters that brought up their little families, in the mouths of the sunken cannon of the French frigates; of the great sharks that were sometimes caught in the meshes of the set-nets! "There was one shark," said our host, another old fisherman, who, by the way, wore a red skull-cap like a cardinal, and had a habit of bobbing his head as he spoke, so as to put one continually in mind of a gigantic woodpecker—"there was one shark I mind particular. My two boys and me was hauling in the net, and soon as I felt it, says I, 'Boys, here's something more than common.' So we all hauled away, and O my! didn't the water boil when he come up? Such a time! Fortnatly, he come up tail first. Lord, if he'd a come up head first he'd a bit the boat in two at one bite! He was all hooked in, and twisted up with the net. I s'pose he had forty hooks in him; and when he got his head above water, he was took sick, and such a time as he had! He must a' vomited up about two barrels of bait—true as I set here. Well, as soon as he got over that, then he tried to get his head around to bite! Lord, if he'd got his head round, he'd a bit the boat in two, and we had it right full of fish, for we'd been out all day with hand-lines. He had a nose in front of his gills just like a duck, only it was nigh upon six feet long."

"It must have been a shovel-nose shark," said Picton.

"That's what a captain of a coaster told me," replied Red-Cap; "he said it must a been a shovel-nose. If he'd only got that shovel-nose turned around, he'd a shovelled us into eternity, fish and all."

"What prevented him getting his head around?" said Picton.

"Why, sir, I took two half-hitches round his tail, soon as I see him come up. And I tell ye when I make two half-hitches, they hold; ask captain there, if I can't make hitches as will hold. What say, captain?"

Captain assented with a confirmatory nod.

"What did you do then?" said Picton. "Did you get him ashore?"

"Get him ashore?" muttered Red-Cap, covering his mouth with one broad brown hand to muffle a contemptuous laugh; "get him ashore! why, we was pretty well off shore for such a sail."

"You might have rowed him ashore," said Picton.

"Rowed him ashore?" echoed Red-Cap, with another contemptuous smile under the brown hand; "rowed him ashore?"

The traveller, finding he was in deep water, answered: "Yes; that is, if you were not too far out."

"A little too far out," replied Red-Cap; "why if I had been a hundred yards only from shore, it would ha' been too far to row, or sail in, with that shovel-nose, without counting the set-nets."

"And what did you do?" said Picton, a little nettled.

"Why," said Red-Cap, "I had to let him go, but first I cut out his liver, and that I did bring ashore, although it filled my boat pretty well full. You can judge how big it was: after I brought it ashore I lay it out on the beach and we measured it, Mr. McAlpin and me, and he'll tell you so too; we laid it out on the beach, that ere liver, and it measured seventeen feet, and then we didn't measure all of it."

"Why the devil," said Picton, "didn't you measure all of it?"

"Well," replied Red-Cap, "because we hadn't a measure long enough."

Meantime the good lady of the hutch was busy arranging some tumblers on the table, and to our great surprise and delight a huge yellow pitcher of milk soon made its appearance, and immediately after an old-fashioned iron bake-pan, with an upper crust of live embers and ashes, was lifted off the chimney trammel, and when it was opened, the fragrance of hot ginger-bread filled the apartment. Then Red-Cap bobbed away at a corner cupboard, until he extracted therefrom a small keg or runlet of St. Croix rum of most ripe age and choice flavor, some of which, by an adroit and experienced crook of the elbow, he managed to insinuate into the milk, which, with a little brown sugar, he stirred up carefully and deliberately with a large spoon, Picton and I watching the proceedings with intense interest. Then the punch was poured out and handed around; while the good wife made little trips from guest to guest with a huge platter filled with the brown and fragrant pieces of the cake, fresh from the bake-pan. And so the baby having subsided (our baby of the "Balaklava"), and the twilight having given place to a grand moonlight on the bay, and the fire sending out its beams of warmth and happiness, glittering on the utensils of the dresser, and tenderly touching with rosy light the cheeks of the small, white-headed fishermen on the margin of the patchwork quilt; while there was no lack of punch and hospitality in the yellow pitcher, who shall say that we were not as well off in the fisherman's hutch as in a grand saloon, surrounded with frescoes and flunkeys, and served with thin lemonade upon trays of silver?

I do not know why it is, but there always has been something very attractive to me in the faces of children; I love to read the physiognomy of posterity, and so get a history of the future world in miniature, before the book itself is fairly printed. And insomuch as Nova Scotia and Newfoundland are said to be the nurseries of England's seamen, it was with no little interest that I caught a glimpse of two boys, one thirteen, the other eleven years old, the eldest children of our friend Red-Cap.

They came in just as we entered the hutch, and quietly seated themselves together by the corner of the fire-place, after modestly shaking hands with all the guests. They were dressed in plain home-spun clothes, with something of a sailor rig, especially the neat check shirts, and old-fashioned, little, low-quartered, round-toed shoes, such as are always a feature in the melo-drama where

Jack plays a part. It is not usual, too, to see such stocky, robust frames as these fisher-boys presented; and in all three, in the father and his two sons, was one general, pervading idea of cleanliness and housewifery. And then, to notice the physiognomy again, each small face, though modest as that of no girl which I could recall at the moment, had its own tale of hardihood to tell; there was a something that recalled the open sea, written in either countenance; courage and endurance; faith and self-reliance; the compass and the rudder; speaking plainly out under each little thatch of white hair. And indeed, as we found out afterwards, those young countenances told the truth; those fisher-boys were Red-Cap's only boat-crew. In all weathers, in all seasons, by night and by day, the three were together, the parent and his two children, upon the perilous deep.

"If I were the father of those boys," I whispered to Red-Cap, "I would be proud of them."

"Would ye?" said he, with a proud, fatherly glance towards them; "well, I thought so once mysel'; it was when a schooner got ashore out there on the rocks; and we could see her, just under the lights of the lighthouse, pounding away; and by reason of the ice, nobody would venture; so my boys said, says they, 'Father, we can go, any way.' So I wouldn't stop when they said that, and so we laid beside the schooner and took off all her crew pretty soon, and they mostly dead with the cold; but it was an awful bad night, what with the darkness and the ice. Yes," he added, after a pause, "they are good boys now; but they won't be with me many years."

"And why not?" I inquired, for I could not see that the young Red-Caps exhibited any migratory signs of their species to justify the remark.

"Because all our boys go to the States just as soon as they get old enough."

"To the States!" I echoed with no little surprise; "why, I thought they all entered the British Navy, or something of that kind."

"Lord bless ye," said Red-Cap, "not one of them. Enter the British Navy! Why, man, you get the whole of our young people. What would they want to enter the British Navy for, when they can enter the United States of America?"

"The air of Cape Breton is certainly favorable to health," said I, in a whisper, to Picton; "look, for example, at the mistress of the hutch!" and so surely as I have a love of womanity, so surely I intended to convey a sentiment of admiration in the brief words spoken to Picton. The wife of *Bonnet Rouge* was at least not young, but her cheek was smooth, and flushed with the glow of health; her eyes liquid and bright; her hair brown, and abundant; her step light and elastic. Although neither Picton, captain, or anybody else in the hutch would remind one of the Angel Raphael, yet Mrs. Red-Cap, as

——"With dispatchful looks, in hasteShe turned, on hospitable thoughts intent,"

was somewhat suggestive of Eve; her movements were grand and simple; there was a welcome in her face that dimpled in and out with every current topic; a Miltonic grandeur in her air, whether she walked or waited. I could not help but admire her, as I do everything else noble and easily understood. Mrs. Red-Cap was a splendid woman; the wife of a fisherman, with an unaffected grace beyond the reach of art, and poor old Louisburgh was something to speak of. Picton expressed his admiration in stronger and profaner language.

We were not the only guests at Red-Cap's. The lighthouse keeper, Mr. Kavanagh, a bachelor and scholar, with his sister, had come down to take a moonlight walk over the heather; for in new Scotland as in old Scotland, the bonny heather blooms, although not so much familiarized there by song and story. But we shall visit lighthouse Point anon, and spend some hours with the two Kavanaghs. Forthright, into the teeth of the harbor, the wind is blowing: "The wind bloweth where it listeth, and thou nearest the sound therof, but canst not tell whence it cometh, and whither it goeth." How long the "Balaklava" may stay here is yet uncertain. So, with a good-night to the Red-Caps and their guests, we once more bear away for the cabin of the schooner and another night's discomfort.

As I have said before in other words, this province is nothing more than a piece of patchwork, intersected with petty boundary lines, so that every nation is stitched in and quilted in spots, without any harmony, or coherence, or general design. The people of Louisburgh are a kind, hospitable, pleasant people, tolerably well informed for the inhabitants of so isolated a corner of the world; but a few miles further off we come upon a totally different race: a canting, covenanting, oat-eating, money-griping, tribe of second-hand Scotch Presbyterians: a transplanted, degenerate, barren patch of high cheek-bones and red hair, with nothing cleaving to them of the original stock, except covetousness and that peculiar cutaneous eruption for which the mother country is celebrated. But we shall soon have enough of these Scotsmen, good reader. Our present visit is to Lighthouse Point, to look out upon the broad Atlantic, the rocky coast, and the island battery, which a century since gave so much trouble to our filibustering fathers of New England. As we walked towards the lighthouse over the pebbly beach that borders the green turf, Picton suddenly starts off and begins a series of great jumps on the turf, giving with every grasshopper-leap a sort of interjectional "Whuh! whuh!" as though the feat was not confined to the leg-muscles only, but included also a necessary exercise of the lungs. And although we shouted at the traveller, he kept on towards the lighthouse, uttering with every jump, "Heather, heather." At last he came to, beside a group of evergreens, and grew rational. The springy, elastic sod, the heather of old Scotland, reproduced in new Scotland, had reminded him of reels and strathspeys, "for," said he, "nobody can walk upon this sort of thing without feeling a desire to dance upon it. Thunder and turf! if we only had the pipes now!"

And sure enough here was the heather; the soft, springy turf, which has made even Scotchmen affectionate. I do not wonder at it; it answers to the foot-step like an echo, as the string of an instrument answers its concord; as love answers love in unison. I do not wonder that Scotchmen love the heather; I am only surprised that so much heather should be wasted on Scotchmen.

We had anticipated a fine marine view from the lighthouse, but in place of it we could only see a sort of semi-luminous vapor, usually called a fog, which enveloped ocean, island, and picturesque coast. We could not discover the Island Battery opposite, which had bothered Sir William in the siege of '45; but nevertheless, we could judge of the difficulty of reaching it with a hostile force, screened as it was by its waves and vapors. The lighthouse is striped with black and white bars, like a zebra, and we entered it. One cannot help but admire such order and neatness, for the lighthouse is a marvel of purity. We were everywhere—in the bed-rooms, in the great lantern with its glittering lamps, in the hall, the parlor, the kitchen; and found in all the same pervading virtue; as fresh and sweet as a bride was that old zebra-striped lighthouse. The Kavanaghs, brother and sister, live here entirely alone; what with books and music, the ocean, the ships, and the sky, they have company enough. One could not help liking them, they have such cheerful faces, and are so kind and hospitable. Good bye, good friends, and peace be with you always! On our route schooner-ward we danced back over the heather, Picton with great joy carrying a small basket filled with his national fruit—a present from the Kavanaghs. What a feast we shall have, fresh fish, lobster, and above all—potatoes!

It is a novel sight to see the firs and spruces on this stormy sea-coast. They grow out, and not up; an old tree spreading over an area of perhaps twenty feet in diameter, with the inevitable spike of green in its centre, and that not above a foot and a half from the ground. The trees in this region are possessed of extraordinary sagacity; they know how hard the wind blows at times, and therefore put forth their branches in full squat, just like country girls at a pic-nic.

On Sunday the wind is still ahead, and Picton and I determine to abandon the "Balaklava." How long she may yet remain in harbor is a matter of fate; so, with brave, resolute hearts, we start off for a five-mile walk, to McGibbet's, the only owner of a horse and wagon in the vicinity of Louisburgh. Squirrels, robins, and rabbits appear and disappear in the road as we march forwards. The country is wild, and in its pristine state; nature everywhere. Now a brook, now a tiny lake, and "the murmuring pines and the hemlocks." At last we arrive at the house of McGibbet, and encounter new Scotland in all its original brimstone and oatmeal.

CHAPTER VIII.

A Blue-Nosed Pair of the most Cerulean Hue—Prospects of a Hard Bargain—Case of Necessity—Romantic Lake with an Unromantic Name—The Discussion concerning Oatmeal—Danger of the Gasterophili—McGibbet makes a Proposition—Farewell to the "Balaklava"—A Midnight Journey—Sydney—Boat Excursion to the Mic Macs—Picton takes off his Mackintosh.

Some learned philosopher has asserted that when a person has become accustomed to one peculiar kind of diet, it will be expressed in the lineaments of his face. How much the constant use of oatmeal could produce such an effect, was plainly visible in the countenances of McGibbet and his lady-love. Both had an unmistakable equine cast; McGibbet, wild, scraggy, and scrubby, with a tuft on his poll that would not have been out of place between the ears of a plough-horse, stared at us, just as such an animal would naturally over the top of a fence; while his gentle mate, who had more of the amiable draught-horse in her aspect, winked at us with both eyes from under a close-crimped frill, that bore a marvellous resemblance to a head-stall. The pair had evidently just returned from kirk. To say nothing of McGibbet's hat, and his wife's shawl, on a chair, and his best boots on the hearth (for he was walking about in his stockings), there was a dry *preceese* air about them, which plainly betokened they were newly stiffened up with the moral starch of the conventicle, and were therefore well prepared to drive a hard bargain for a horse and wagon to Sydney. But what surprised me most of all was the imperturbable coolness of Picton. Without taking a look scarcely at the persons he was addressing, the traveller stalked in with an—"I say, we want a horse and wagon to Sydney; so look sharp, will you, and turn out the best thing you have here?"

The moral starch of the conventicle stiffened up instantly. Like the blacksmith of Cairnvreckan, who, as a *professor*, would drive a nail for no man on the Sabbath or kirk-fast, unless in a case of absolute necessity, and then always charged an extra saxpence for each shoe; so it was plain to be seen that McGibbet had a conscience which required to be pricked both with that which knows no law, and the saxpence extra. He turned to his wife and addressed her in Gaelic! Then we knew what was coming.

Mrs. McGibbet opened the subject by saying that they were both accustomed to the observance of the Sabbath, and that "she didn't think it was right for man to transgress, when the law was so plain"——

Here McGibbet broke in and said that—"He was free to confess he had commeeted a grreat menny theengs kwhich were a grreat deal worse than Sabbath-breaking."

Upon which Mrs. McG. interrupted him in turn with a few words, which, although in Gaelic, a language we did not understand, conveyed the impression that she was not addressing her liege lord in the language of endearment, and again continued in English: "That it was held sinful in the community to wark or do anything o' the sort, or to fetch or carry even a sma bundle"——

"For kwich," said McGibbet, "is a fine to be paid to the meenister, of five shillins currency"——

Here Picton stopped whistling a bar of "Bonny Doon," and observed to me: "About a dollar of your money. We'll pay the fine."

"Yes," chimed in McGibbet, "a dollar"——and was again stopped by his wife, who raised her eyebrows to the borders of her kirk-frill and brought them down vehemently over her blue eyes at him.

"Or to travel the road," she said, "even on foot, to say nothing of a wagon and horse."

"But," interrupted Picton, "my dear madam, we must get on, I tell you; I must be inSydney to-morrow, to catch the steamer for St. John's."

At this observation of the traveller the pair fell back upon their Gaelic for a while, and in the meantime Picton whispered me: "I see; they want to raise the price on us: but we won't give in; they'll be sharp enough after the job by and by."

The pair turned towards us and both shook their heads. It was plain to be seen the conference had not ended in our favor.

"Ye see," said the gude-wife, "we are accustomed to the observance of the Sabbath, and would na like to break it, except"—

"In a case of necessity; you are perfectly right," chimed in Picton; "I agree with you myself. Now this is a case of necessity; here we are; we must get on, you see; if we don't get on we miss the steamer to-morrow for St. John's—she only runs once a fortnight there—it's plain enough a clear case of necessity; it's like," continued Picton, evidently trying to corner some authority in his mind, "it's like—let me see—it's like—a—pulling—a sheep out of a ditch—a—which they always do on the Sabbath, you know, to a—get us on to Sydney."

Both McGibbet and his wife smiled at Picton's ingenuity, but straightway put on the equine look again. "It might be so; but it was clean contrary to their preenciples."

"I'll be hanged," whispered Picton, "if I offer more than the usual price, which I heard at Louisburgh was one pound ten, to Sydney, and the fine extra. I see what they are after."

There was an awkward pause in the negotiations. McGibbet scratched his poll, and looked wistfully at his wife, but the kirk-frill was stiffened up with the moral starch, as aforesaid.

Suddenly, Picton looked out of the window. "By Jove!" said he, "I think the wind is changed! After all, we may get around in the 'Balaklava.'"

McGibbet looked somewhat anxiously out of the window also, and grunted out a little more Gaelic to his love. The kirk-frill relented a trifle.

"Perhaps the gentlemen wad like a glass of milk after thae long walk? And Robert" (which she pronounced Robbut), "a bit o' the corn-cake."

Upon which Robbut, with great alacrity, turned towards the bed-room, from whence he brought forth a great white disk, that resembled the head of a flour-barrel, but which proved to be a full-grown griddle cake of corn-meal. This, with the pure milk, from the cleanest of scoured pans, was acceptable enough after the long walk.

We had observed some beautiful streams, and blue glimpses of lakes on the road to McGibbet's, and just beyond his house was a larger lake, several miles in extent, with picturesque hills on either side, indented-with coves, and studded with islands, sometimes stretching away to distant slopes of green turf, and sometimes reflecting masses of precipitous rock, crowned with the spiry tops of spruces and firs. Indeed, all the country around, both meadow and upland, was very pleasing to the sight. A low range of hills skirted the northern part of what seemed to be a spacious, natural amphitheatre, while on the south side a diversity of highlands and water added to the whole the charm of variety.

"You have a fine country about you, Mr. McGibbet," said I.

"Ay," he replied.

"And what is it called here?"

"We ca' it Get-Along!" said Robbut, with an intensely Scotch accent on the "Get."

"And yonder beautiful lake—what is the name of that?" said I, in hopes of taking refuge behind something more euphonious.

"Oh! ay," replied he, "that's just Get-Along, too. We doan't usually speak of it, but whan we do, we just ca' it Get-Along Lake, and it's not good for much."

I thought it best to change the subject. "Do you like this as well as the oat-cake?" said I, with my mouth full of the dry, husky provender.

"Nae," said McGibbet, with an equine shake of the head, "it's not sae fellin."

Not so filling! Think of that, ye pampered minions of luxury, who live only upon delicate viands; who prize food, not as it useful, but as it is tasteful; who can even encourage a depraved, sensual appetite so far as to appreciate flavor; who enjoy meats, fish, and poultry, only as they minister to your palates; who flirt with spring-chickens and trifle with sweet-breads in wanton indolence, without a thought of your cubic capacity; without a reflection that you can live just as well upon so many square inches of oatmeal a day as you can upon the most elaborate French kickshaws; nay, that you can be elevated to the level of a scientific problem, and work out your fillings, with nothing to guide you but a slate and pencil!

"Then you like oatmeal better than this?" said Picton, soothing down a husky lump, with a cup of milk.

"Ay," responded McGibbet.

"And you always eat it, whenever you can get it, I suppose?" continued Picton, with a most innocent air.

"Ay," responded McGibbet.

"I should think some of you Scotchmen would be afraid of contracting a disease that is engendered in the system by the use of this sort of grain. I hope, Mr. McGibbet," said Picton, with imperturbable coolness, "you keep clear of the bots, and that sort of thing, you know?"

"Kwat?" said Robbut, with the most startled, horse-like look he had yet put on.

"The gasterophili," replied Picton, "which I would advise you to steer clear of, if you want to live long."

As this was a word with too many gable-ends for Robbut's comprehension, he only responded by giving such a smile as a man might be expected to give who had his mouth full of aloes, and as the conversation was wandering off from the main point, addressed himself to Mrs. McG. in the vernacular again.

"We would like to obleege ye," said the lady, "if it was not for the transgression; and we do na like to break the Sabbath for ony man."

"Although," interposed Robbut, "I am free to confess that I have done a great many things worse than breakin' the Sabbath."

"But if to-morrow would do as well," resumed his wife, "Robbut would take ye to Sydney."

To this Picton shook his head. "Too late for the steamer."

"Or to-night; I wad na mind that," said the pious Robbut, "*if it was after dark*, and that will bring ye to Sydney before the morn."

"That will do," said Picton, slapping his thigh. "Lend us your horse and wagon to go down to the schooner and get our luggage; we will be back this evening, and then go on to Sydney, eh? That will do; a ride by moonlight;" and the traveller jumped up from his seat, walked with great strides towards the fire-place, turned his back to the blaze, hung a coat-tail over each arm, and whistled "Annie Laurie" at Mrs. McGibbet.

The suggestion of Picton meeting the views of all concerned, the diplomacy ended. Robbut put himself in his Sunday boots, and hitched up a spare rib of a horse before a box-wagon without springs, which he brought before the door with great complacency. The traveller and I were soon on the ground-floor of the vehicle, seated upon a log of wood by way of cushion; and with a chirrup from McGibbet, off we went. At the foot of the first hill, our horse stopped; in vain Picton jerked at the rein, and shouted at him: not a step further would he go, until Robbut himself came down to the rescue. "Get along, Boab!" said his master; and Bob, with a mute, pitiful appeal in his countenance, turned his face towards salt-water. At the foot of the next hill he stopped again, when the irascible Picton jumped out, and with one powerful twitch of the bridle, gave Boab such a hint to "get on," that it nearly jerked his head off. And Boab did get on, only to stop at the ascent of the next hill. Then we began to understand the tactics of the animal. Boab had been the only conveyance between Louisburgh and Sydney for many years, and, as he was usually over-burdened, made a point to stop at the up side of every hill on the road, to let part of his freight get out and walk to the top of the acclivity with him. So, by way of compromise, we made a feint of getting out at every rise of ground, and Boab, who always turned his head around at each stopping-place, seemed to be satisfied with the observance of the ceremony, and trotted gaily forward. At last we came to a place we had named Sebastopol in the morning—a great sharp edge of rock as high as a man's waist, that cut the road in half, over which we lifted the wagon, and were soon in view of the bright little harbor and the "Balaklava" at anchor. Mr. McAlpin kindly gave quarters to our steed in his out-house, and offered to raise a signal for the schooner to send a boat ashore. As he was Deputy United States Consul, and as I was tired of the red-cross of St. George, I asked him to hoist his consular flag. Up to the flag-staff truck rose the roll of white and red worsted, then uncoiled, blew out, and the blessed stars and stripes were waving over me. It is surprising to think how transported one can be sometimes with a little bit of bunting!

And now the labor of packing commenced, of which Picton had the greatest share by far; the little cabin of the schooner was pretty well spread out with his traps on every side; and this being ended, Picton got out his travelling-organ and blazed away in a *finale* of great tunes and small, sometimes fast, sometimes slow, as the humor took him. After all, we parted from the jolly little craft with regret: our trunks were lowered over the side; we shook hands with all on board; and were rowed in silence to the land.

I have had some experience in travelling, and have learned to bear with ordinary firmness and philosophy the incidental discomforts one is certain to meet with on the road; but I must say, the discipline already acquired had not prepared me for the unexpected appearance of our wagon after Picton's luggage was placed in it. First, two solid English trunks of sole-leather filled the bottom of the vehicle; then the traveller's Minié-rifle, life-preserver, strapped-up blankets, and hand-bag were stuffed in the sides: over these again were piled my trunk and the traveller's valise (itself a monster of straps and sole-leather); then again his portable-secretary and the hand-organ in a box. These made such a pyramid of luggage, that riding ourselves was out of the question. What with the trunks and the cordage to keep them staid, our wagon looked like a ship of the desert. To crown all, it began to rain steadily. "Now, then," said Picton, climbing up on his confounded travelling equipage, "let's get on." With some difficulty I made a half-seat on the corner of my own trunk; Picton shouted out at Boab; the Newfoundland sailors who had brought us ashore, put their shoulders to the wheels, and away we went, waving our hats in answer to the hearty cheers of the sailors. It was down hill from McAlpin's to the first bridge, and so far we had nothing to care for, except to keep a look-out we were not shaken off our high perch. But at the foot of the first hill Boab stopped! In vain Picton shouted at him to get on; in vain he shook rein and made a feint of getting down from the wagon. Boab was not intractable, but he was sagacious; he had been fed on that sort of chaff too long. Picton and I were obliged to humor his prejudices, and dismount in the mud, and after one or two feeble attempts at a ride, gave it up, walked down hill and up, lifted the wagon by inches over Sebastopol, and finally arrived at McGibbet's, wet, tired, and hungry. That Sabbath-broker received us with a grim smile of satisfaction, put on the half-extinguished fire the smallest bit of wood he could find in the pile beside the hearth, and then went away with Boab to the stable. "Gloomy prospects ahead, Picton!" The traveller said never a word.

Now I wish to record here this, that there is no place, no habitation of man, however humble, that cannot be lighted up with a smile of welcome, and the good right-hand of hospitality, and made cheerful as a palace hung with the lamps of Aladdin!

McGibbet, after leading his beast to the stable, returned, and warming his wet hands at the fire, grunted out; "It rains the nigcht."

"Yes," answered Picton, hastily, "rains like blue blazes: I say, get us a drop of whisky, will you?"

To this the equine replied by folding his hands one over the other with a saintly look. "I never keep thae thing in the hoose."

"Picton," said I, "if we could only unlash our luggage, I have a bottle of capital old brandy in my trunk, but it's too much trouble."

"Oh! na," quoth Robbut with a most accommodating look, "it will be nae trooble to get to it."

"Well, then," said Picton, "look sharp, will you?" and our host, with great swiftness, moved off to the wagon, and very soon returned with the trunk on his shoulder, according to directions.

"But," said I, taking out the bottle of precious fluid, "here it is, corked up tight, and what is to be done for a cork-screw?"

"I've got one," said the saint.

"I thought it was likely," quoth Picton, drily; "look sharp, will you?"

And Robbut did look sharp, and produced the identical instrument before Picton and I had exchanged smiles. Then Robbut spread out three green tumblers on the table, and following Picton's lead, poured out a stout half-glass, at which I shouted out, "Hold up!" for I thought he was filling the tumbler for my benefit. It proved to be a mistake; Robbut stopped for a moment, but instantly recovering himself, covered the tumbler with his four fingers, and, to use a Western phrase, "got outside of the contents quicker than lightning." Then he brought from his bed-room a coarse sort of worsted horse-blanket, and with a "Ye'll may-be like to sleep an hour or twa?" threw down his family-quilt and retired to the arms of Mrs. McG. Picton gave a great crunching blow with his boot-heel at the back-stick, and laid on a good supply of fuel. We were wet through and through, but we wrapped ourselves in our travelling-blankets like a brace of clansmen in their plaids, put our feet towards the niggardly blaze, and were soon bound and clasped with sleep.

At two o'clock our host roused us from our hard bed, and after a stretch, to get the stiffness out of joints and muscles, we took leave of the Presbyterian quarters. The day was just dawning: at this early hour, lake and hill-side, tree and thicket, were barely visible in the grey twilight. The wagon, with its pyramid of luggage, moved off in the rain, McGibbet walking beside Boab, and Picton and I following after, with all the gravity of chief mourners at a funeral. To give some idea of the road we were upon, let it be understood, it had once been an old *French* military road, which, after the destruction of the fortress of Louisburgh, had been abandoned to the British Government and the elements. As a consequence, it was embroidered with the ruts and gullies of a century, the washing of rains, and the tracks of wagons; howbeit, the only traverse upon it in later years were the wagon of McGibbet and the saddle-horse of the post-rider. "Get-Along" had a population of seven hundred Scotch Presbyters, and therefore it will be easy to understand the condition of its turnpike.

Up hill and down hill, through slough and over rock, we trudged, for mile after mile. Sometimes beside Get-Along Lake, with its grey, spectral islands and woodlands; sometimes by rushing brooks and dreary farm-fields; now in paths close set with evergreens; now in more open grounds, skirted with hills and dotted with silent, two-penny cottages. Sometimes Picton mounted his pyramid of trunk-leather for a mile or so of nods; sometimes I essayed the high perch, and holding on by a cord, dropped off in a moment's forgetfulness, with the constant fear of waking up in a mud-hole, or under the wagon-wheels. But even these respites were brief. It is not easy to ride up hill and down by rock and rut, under such conditions. We were very soon convinced it was best to leave the wagon to its load of sole-leather, and walk through the mud to Sydney.

After mouldy Halifax, and war-worn Louisburgh, the little town of Sydney is a pleasant rural picture. Everybody has heard of the Sydney coal-mines: we expected to find the miner's finger-marks everywhere; but instead of the smoky, sulphurous atmosphere, and the black road, and the sulky, grimy, brick tenements, we were surprised with clean, white, picket-fences; and green lawns, and clever, little cottages, nestled in shrubbery and clover. The mines are over the bay, five miles from South Sydney. Slowly we dragged on, until we came to a sleepy little one-story inn, with supernatural dormer windows rising out of the roof, before which Boab stopped. We *paid* McGibbet's kirk-fine, wagon-fare, and his unconscionable charge for his conscience, without parleying with him; we were too sleepy to indulge in the luxury of a monetary skirmish. A pretty, red-cheeked chambermaid, with lovely drooping eyes, showed us to our rooms; it was yet very early in the morning; we were almost ashamed to get into bed with such dazzling white sheets after the dark-brown accommodations of the "Balaklava;" but we did get in, and slept; oh! how sweetly! until breakfast at one!

"Twenty-four miles of such foot-travel will do pretty well for an invalid, eh, Picton?"

"All serene?" quoth the traveller, interrogatively.

"Feel as well as ever I did in my life," said I, with great satisfaction.

"Then let's have a bath," and, at Picton's summons, the chambermaid brought up in our rooms two little tubs of fair water, and a small pile of fat, white napkins. The bathing over, and the outer men new clad, "from top to toe," down we went to the cosy parlor to breakfast; and such a breakfast!

I tell you, my kind and gentle friend; *you*, who are now reading this paragraph, that here, as in all other parts of the world, there are a great many kinds of people; only that here, in Nova Scotia, the difference is in spots, not in individuals. And I will venture to say to those philanthropists who are eternally preaching "of the masses," and "to the masses," that here "masses" can be found—concrete "masses," not yet individualized: as ready to jump after a leader as a flock of sheep after a bell-wether; only that at every interval of five or ten miles between place and place in Nova Scotia, they are apt to jump in contrary directions. There are Scotch Nova Scotiaites even in Sydney. Otherwise the place is marvellously pleasant.

I must confess that I had a romantic sort of idea in visiting Sydney; a desire to return by way of the *Bras d'Or* lake, the "arm of gold," the inland sea of Cape Breton, that makes the island itself only a border for the water in its interior. And as the navigation is frequently performed by the Micmac Indians, in their birch-bark canoes, I determined to be a *voyageur* for the nonce, and engage a couple of Micmacs to paddle me homewards, at least one day's journey. The wigwams of the tribe were pitched about a mile from the town, and I proposed a visit to their camp as an afternoon's amusement. Picton readily assented, and down we went to the wharf, where the landlady assured us we would find some of the tribe. These Indians, often expert coopers, are employed to barrel up fish; the busy wharf was covered with laborers, hard at work, heading and hooping ship loads of salt mackerel; and among the workmen were some with the unmistakable lozenge eyes, high cheek-bones, and rhubarb complexion of the native

American. Upon inquiry, we were introduced to one of the Rhubarbarians. He was a little fellow, not in leggings and quill-embroidered hunting-shirt, with belt of wampum and buckskin moccasins; armed with bow and arrow, tomahawk and scalping-knife; such as one would expect to navigate a wild, romantic lake with, in birch-bark canoe; but a pinched-up specimen of a man, in a seedy black suit, out of which rose a broad, flat face, like the orb of a sun-flower, bearing one side the aboriginal black eye, and on the other the civilized, surrounded with the blue and purple halo of battle. We had barely opened our business with the Indian, when a bonny Scotchman, a fellow-cooper of salt mackerel, introduced himself:

"Oh, ye visit the Micmacs the day?"

No answer.

"De'il a canoe has he to tak ye there" (the Indian slunk away), "but I'll tak ye tull 'em for one and saxpence, in a gude boat."

The fellow had such an honest face, and the offer was so fair and earnest, that Picton's and my own trifling prejudices were soon overcome, and we directed Malcolm, for that was his name, to bring his boat under the inn-windows after the dinner-hour. I regret to say that we found Malcolm tolerably drunk after dinner, with a leaky boat, under the inn-windows. And farther, I am pained to state the national characteristic was developed in Malcolm drunk, from which there was no appeal to Malcolm sober, for he insisted upon double fare, and time was pressing. To this we assented, after a brief review of former prejudices. We got in the boat and put off. We had barely floated away into the beautiful landscape when a fog swept over us, and Malcolm's nationality again woke up. He would have four times as much as he had charged in the first instance, or "he'd tak us over, and land us on the ither side of the bay."

Then Picton's nationality woke up, and he unbuttoned his mackintosh. "Now, sir," said he to Malcolm, as he rose from his seat in the boat, his head gracefully inclined towards his starboard shirt-collar, and his two tolerably large fists arrayed in order of battle within a few brief inches of the delinquent's features, "did I understand you to say that you had some idea of taking this gentleman and myself to the other side of the bay?"

There was a boy in our boat—a fair-haired, blue-eyed representative of Nova Scotia; a sea-boy, with a dash of salt-water in his ruddy cheeks, who had modestly refrained from taking part in the dispute.

"Come, now," said he to Malcolm, "pull away, and let us get the gentlemen up to the camp," and he knit his boy brow with determination, as if he meant to have it settled according to contract.

"Yes," said Picton, nodding at the boy, "and if he don't"——

"I'm pullin' an't I?" quoth the descendant of King Duncan, a little frightened, and suiting the action to the word; "I'm a-pewlin," and here his oar missed the water, and over he tumbled with a great splash in the bottom of the boat. "I'm a-pewlin," he whined, as he regained his seat and the oar, "and all I want is to hae my honest airnins."

"Then pull away," said Picton, as he resumed his seat in the stern-sheets.

"Ay," quoth the Scotchman, "I know the Micmacs weel, and thae squaws too; deil a one o' 'em but knows Malcolm"——

"Pull away," said the boy.

"They are guid-lookin', thae squaws, and I'm a bachelter; and I tell ye when I tak ye tull em—for I know the hail o' em—if ye are gentlemen, ye'll pay me my honest airnins."

"And I tell you," answered Picton, his fist clenched, his eye flashing again, and his indignant nostrils expressing a degree of anger language could not express; "I tell you, if you do not carry us to the Micmac camp without further words, I'll pay you your honest earnings before you get there: I'll punch that Scotch head of yours till it looks like a photograph!"[Pg 176]

CHAPTER IX.

The Micmac Camp—Indian Church-warden and Broker—Interior of a Wigwam—A Madonna—A Digression—Malcolm discharged—An Indian Bargain—The Inn Parlor, and a Comfortable Night's Rest.

The threat had its effect: in a few minutes our boat ran bows-on up the clear pebbled beach before the Micmac camp.

It was a little cluster of birch-bark wigwams, pitched upon a carpet of greensward, just at the edge of one of the loveliest harbors in the world. The fog rolled away like the whiff of vapor from a pipe, and melted out of sight. Before us were the blue and violet waters, tinged with the hues of sunset, the rounded, swelling, curving shores opposite, dotted with cottages; the long, sweeping, creamy beaches, the distant shipping, and, beyond, the great waters of the Gulf of St. Lawrence. Nearer at hand were "the murmuring pines and the hemlocks," the tender green light seen in vistas of firs and spruces, the thin smoke curling up from the wigwams, the birch-bark canoes, the black, bright eyes of the children, the sallow faces of the men, and the pretty squaws, arrayed in blue broad-cloth frocks and leggings, and modesty, and moccasins.

"Now, here we are," said Malcolm, triumphantly, "and wha d'ye thenk o' the Micmacs? Deil a wan o' the yellow deevils but knows Malcolm, an I'll introjewce ye to the hail o' em."

"Stop, sir," said Picton, sternly, "we want none of your company. You can take your boat back," (here I nodded affirmatively), "and we'll walk home."

It was quite a picture, that of our oarsman, upon this summons to depart. He had just laid his hand upon the shoulder of a fat, good-natured looking squaw, to commence the introjewcing; one foot rested on the bottom of an overturned canoe, in an attitude of command; his old battered tarpaulin hat, his Guernsey shirt, and salt-mackerel trowsers, finely relieved against the violet-tinted water; but oh! how chop-fallen were those rugged features under that old tarpaulin!

The scene had its effect; I am sure Picton and myself would gladly have paid the quadruple sum on the spot—after all, it was but a trifle—for we both drew forth a sovereign at the same moment.

Unfortunately Malcolm had no change; not a "bawbee." "Then," said we, "go back to the inn, and we'll pay you on our return."

"And," said Malcolm, in an unearthly whine that might have been heard all over the camp, "d' ye get me here to take advantage o' me, and no pay me my honest airnins?"

"What the devil to do with this fellow, short, of giving him a drubbing, I do not know," said Picton. "Here, you, give us change for a sovereign, or take yourself off and wait at the hotel till we get back again."

"I canna change a sovereign, I tell ye"——

"Then be off with you, and wait."

"Wad ye send me away without my honest airnins?" he uttered, with a whine like the bleat of a bagpipe.

Picton drew a little closer to Malcolm, with one fist carefully doubled up and put in ambush behind his back. But the boy interposed—"Perhaps the Micmac chief could change the sovereign."

"Oh! ay," quoth Malcolm, who had given an uneasy look at Picton as he stepped towards him; "Oh! ay; I'se tak ye tull 'im;" and without further ado he stepped off briskly towards the centre of the camp, and we followed in his wake. When our file-leader reached the wigwam of the chief, he went down on hands and knees, lifted up a little curtain or blanket in front of the low door of the tent, crawled in head first, and we followed close upon his heels.

As soon as the eye became accustomed to the dim and uncertain light of the interior, we began to examine the curious and simple architecture of this human bee-hive. A circle of poles, say about ten feet in diameter at the base, and tied together to an apex at the top, covered with the thin bark of the birch-tree, except a space above to let out the smoke, was all the protection these people had against the elements in summer or winter. The floor, of course, was the primitive soil of Cape Breton; in the centre of the tent a few sticks were smouldering away over a little pile of ashes: the thin smoke lifted itself up in folds of blue vapor until it stole forth into the evening air from the opening in the roof. Through this aperture the light—the only light of the tent—fell down upon the group below: the old chief with his great silver cross, and medal, and snow-white hair; the young and beautiful squaw with her pappoose at the breast, like a Madonna by Murillo; Malcolm's battered tarpaulin and Guernsey shirt; and the two unpicturesque objects of the party—Picton and myself. Around the central fire a broad, green border of fragrant hemlock twigs, extending to the skirts of the tent, was raised a few inches from the ground. Upon this couch we sat, and opened our business with the aged sagamore.

Old Indian was very courteous; he drew forth a bag of clinking dollars, for strange as it may seem, he was a churchwarden: the Micmacs being all Catholics, the chief holds the silver keys of St. Peter. But venerable and pious as he appeared, with his silver cross and silver hair, the old fellow was something too of a broker! He demanded a fair rate of commission—eight per cent. premium on every dollar! Even this would not answer our purpose; it was as difficult to make change with the old churchwarden as with Malcolm: there was no money in the camp except hard silver dollars.

No change for a sovereign!

So we went forth from the wigwam again on all fours, and it was only by another promise of a sound drubbing that Malcolm was finally persuaded to drop off and leave us.

Aboriginal certainly is the camp of the Micmacs. The birch-bark wigwams; the canoes that lined the beach; the paddles, the utensils; the bows and arrows; the parti-colored baskets, are independent of, are earlier than our arts and manufactures. So far as these people are concerned, the colonial government has been mild and considerate. Although there are game-laws in the Province, yet Micmac has a privilege no white man can possess. At all seasons he may hunt or fish; he may stick his *aishkun* in the salmon as it runneth up the rivers to spawn, and shoot the partridge on its nest, if he please, without fine and imprisonment. Some may think it better to preserve the game than to preserve the Indian; but some think otherwise. For my part, when the question is between the man and the salmon, I am content to forego fish.

As we walked through the Micmac camp we met our semi-civilized friend with the lozenge eyes, and I made a contract with him for a brief voyage on le Bras d'Or. But alas! Indian will sometimes take a lesson from his white comrades! Micmac's charge at first was one pound for a trip of twenty-four miles on the "Arm of Gold;" cheap enough. But before we left the camp it was two pounds. That I agreed to pay. Then there was a portage of three miles, over which the canoe had to be carried. "Well?" "And it would take two men to paddle." "Well?" "And then the canoe had to be paddled back." "Well?" "And then carried over the portage again." "Well?" "And so it would be four pounds!" Here the negotiations were broken off; how much more it would cost I did not ascertain. The rate of progression was too rapid for further inquiry.

So we walked home again amid the fragrant resinous trees, until we gained the high road, and so by pretty cottages, and lawns, and picket fences; sometimes meeting groups of wandering damsels with their young and happy lovers; sometimes twos and threes of horse-women, in habits, hats, and feathers; now catching a glimpse of the broad, blue harbor; now looking down a green lane, bordered with turf and copse; until we reached our comfortable quarters at Mrs. Hearn's, where the pretty chambermaid, with drooping eyes, welcomed us in a voice whose music was sweeter than the tea-bell she held in her hand. And here, too, we found Malcolm, waiting for his pay, partially sober and quiet as a lamb.

I trust the reader will not find fault with the writer for dwelling upon these minute particulars. In this itinerary of the trip to the Acadian land, I have endeavored to portray, as faithfully as may be, the salient features of the country, and particularly those contrasts visible in the settlements; the jealous preservation of those dear, old, splendid prejudices, that separate tribe from tribe, clan from clan, sect from sect, race from race. I wish the reader to see and know the country as it is, not for the purpose of arousing his prejudices against a neighboring people, but rather with the intent of showing to what result these prejudices tend, in order that he may correct his own. A mere aggregation of tribes is not a great people. Take the human species in a state of sectionalism, and it does not make much difference whether it is in the shape of the Indian, proud of the blue and red stripes on his face, or the Scotchman, proud of the blue and red stripes on his plaid, the inferiority of the human animal, with his tribal sheep-mark on him, is evident enough to any person of enlarged understanding. Therefore I have been minute and faithful in describing the species McGibbet and Malcolm, and in contrasting them with the hardy fisherman of Louisburgh, the Micmacs of Sydney, the negroes of Deer's Castle, the Acadians of Chizzetcook, and as we shall see anon with other sectional specimens, just as they present their kaleidoscopic hues in the local settlements of this colony.

It is just a year since I was seated in that cosy inn-parlor at Sydney, and how strangely it all comes back again: the little window overlooking the harbor, the lights on the twinkling waters;

147

the old-fashioned house-clock in the corner of the room; the bright brass andirons; the cut paper chimney-apron; the old sofa; the cheerful lamp, and the well-polished table. And I remember, too, the happy, tranquil feeling of lying in the snow-white sheets at night, and talking with Picton of our overland journey from Louisburgh; of McGibbet and Malcolm; and then we branched out on the great subject of Indian rights, and Indian wrongs; of squaws and pappooses; of wigwams and canoes, until at last I dropped off in a doze, and heard only a repetition of Micmac—Micmac—Micmac—Mic—Mac——Mic———Mac! To this day I am unable to say whether the sound I heard came from Picton, or the great house-clock in the corner.

CHAPTER X.

Over the Bay—A Gigantic Dumb Waiter—Erebus—Reflections—
White and Black Squares of the Chess-board—Leave-taking—An
Interruption—The Aibstract Preencipels of Feenance.

Bright and early next morning we arose for an expedition across
the bay to North Sydney and the coal-mines. A fresh breakfast
in a sunny room, a brisk walk to the breezy, grass-grown parapet,
that defends the harbor; a thought of the first expedition to lay
down the telegraph line between the old and new hemispheres, for
here lie the coils of the sub-marine cable, as they were left after the
stormy essay of the steamer "James Adger," a year before—what a
theme for a poet!

"Perhaps in this neglected spot is laid.Some spark, now dormant,
of electric fire:News, that the board of brokers might have
swayed,Or broke the banks that trembled with the wire."

—and we take an airy seat on the poop-deck of the little English
steamer, and are wafted across the harbor, five miles, to a small
sea-port, where coal-schutes and railways run out over the wharfs,
and coasters, both fore-and-aft, and square-rigged, are gathered
in profusion. A glass of English ale at a right salt-sea tavern, a
bay horse, and two-wheeled "jumper" for the road, and away we roll
towards the mines. Now up hill and down; now passing another
Micmac camp on the green margin of the beach; now by trim
gardens without flowers; now getting nearer to the mines, which
we know by the increasing blackness of the road; until at last we
bowl past rows of one story dingy tenements of brick, with

149

miners' wives and children clustered about them like funereal flowers; until we see the forges and jets of steam, and davits uplifted in the air; and hear the rattle of the iron trucks and the rush of the coal as it runs through the schutes into the rail-cars on the road beneath. We tie our pony beside a cinder-heap, and mount a ladder to the level of the huge platform above the shaft. A constant supply of small hand-cars come up with demoniac groans and shrieks from the bowels of the earth through the shaft. These are instantly seized by the laborers and run over an iron floor to the schute, where they are caught in titantic trammels, and overturned into harsh thunder. Meanwhile the demon car-bringer has sunk again on its errand; the suspending rope wheeling down with dizzy swiftness. As one car-bearer descends, another rises to the surface with its twin wheel-vessels of coal.

"Would you like to go down?"

"How far down?"

"Sixty fathoms."

Three hundred and sixty feet! Think of being suspended by a thread, from a height twice that of Trinity's spire, and whirled into such a depth by steam! We crawled into the little iron box, just large enough to allow us to sit up with our heads against the top, both ends of our parachute being open; the operator presses down a bar, and instantly the earth and sky disappear, and we are wrapt in utter darkness. Oh? how sickening is this sinking feeling! Down—down—down! What a gigantic dumb-waiter! Down, down, a hot gust of vapor—a stifling sensation—a concussion upon the iron floor at the foot of the shaft; a multitude of twinkling lamps, of fiends, of grimy faces, and no bodies—and we are in a coal-mine.

There was a black, bituminous seat for visitors, sculptured out of the coal, just beyond the shaft, and to this we were led by the carboniferous fiends. My heart beat violently. I do not know how it went with Picton, but we were both silent. Oh! for a glimpse of the blue sky and waving trees above us, and a long breath of fresh air!

As soon as the stifling sensation passed away, we breathed more freely, and the lungs became accustomed to the subterranean atmosphere. In the gloom, we could see the smutted features only, of miners moving about, and to heighten the Dantesque reality, new and strange sounds, from different parts of the enormous cavern, came pouring towards the common centre—the shaft of the coal-pit.

These were the laden cars on the tram-ways, drawn by invisible horses, from the distant works in the mine, rolling and reverberating through the infernal aisles of this devil's cathedral. One could scarcely help recalling the old grandfather of Maud's Lord-lover:

——"lately died,Gone to a *blacker pit,* for whomGrimy nakedness, dragging his trucksAnd laying his trams, *in a poisoned gloom*Wrought, till he crept from a gutted mineMaster of half a servile shire,And left his coal all turned into goldTo a grandson, first of his noble line."

151

Intermingled with these sounds were others, the jar and clash of gateways, the dripping and splashing of water, the rolling thunder of the ascending and descending iron parachutes in the shaft, the trampling of horses, the distant report of powder-blasts, and the shrill jargon of human speakers, near, yet only partially visible.

"Is it a clear day overhead?" said the black bust of one of the miners, with a lamp in its *hat*!

Just think of it! We had only been divorced from the aërial blue of a June sky a minute before. Our very horse was so high above us that we could have distinguished him only by the aid of a telescope—that is, if the solid ribs of the globe were not between us and him.

As soon as we became accustomed to the place, we moved off after the foreman of the mine. We walked through the miry tram-ways under the low, black arches, now stepping aside to let an invisible horse and car, "grating harsh thunder," pass us in the murky darkness; now through a door-way, momently closed to keep the foul and clear airs separate, until we came to the great furnace of the mine that draws off all the noxious vapors from this nest of Beelzebub. Then we went to the stables where countless horses are stalled—horses that never see the light of day again, or if they do, are struck blind by the apparition; now in wider galleries, and new explorations, where we behold the busy miners, twinkling like the distant lights of a city, and hear the thunder-burst, as the blast explodes in the murky chasms. At last, tired, oppressed, and sickened with the vast and horrible prison, for such it seems, we retrace our steps, and once more enter the iron parachute. A touch of the magic lever, and again we fly away; but now upwards, upwards to the glorious blue sky and air of mother earth. A miner with his lamp accompanies us. By its dim light we see how rapidly we spin through the shaft. Our car clashes again at the top, and as we step forth into the clear sunshine, we thank God for such a bright and beautiful world up stairs!

"Do you know," said I, "Picton, what we would do if we had such a devil's pit as that in the States?"

"Well?" answered the traveller, interrogatively.

"We would make niggers work it."

"I dare say," replied Picton, drily and satirically; "but, sir, I am proud to say that our government does not tolerate barbarity; to consign an inoffensive fellow-creature to such horrible labor, merely because he is black, is at variance with the well-known humanity of the whole British nation, sir."

"But those miners, Picton, were black as the devil himself."

"The miners," replied Picton, with impressive gravity, "are black, but not negroes."

"Nothing but mere white people, Picton?"

"Eh?" said the traveller.

"Only white people, and therefore we need not waste one grain of sympathy over a whole pit full of them."

"Why not?"

"Because they are not niggers, what is the use of wasting sympathy upon a rat-hole full of white British subjects?"

"I tell you what it is," said Picton, "you are getting personal."

We were now rolling past the dingy tenements again. Squalid-looking, care-worn women, grimy children:

"To me there's something touching, I confess, In the grave look of early thoughtfulness, Seen often in some little childish face, Among the poor;"—

But these children's faces are not such. A child's face—God bless it! should always have a little sunshine in its glance; but these are mere staring faces, without expression, that make you shudder and feel sad. Miners by birth; human moles fitted to burrow in darkness for a life-time. Is it worth living for? No wonder those swart laborers underground are so grim and taciturn: no wonder there was not a face lighted up by those smoky lamps in the pit, that had one line of human sympathy left in its rigidly engraved features!

But we must have coal, and we must have cotton. The whole plantations of the South barely supply the press with paper; and the messenger of intelligence, the steam-ship, but for coal could not perform its glorious mission. What is to be done, Picton? If every man is willing to give up his morning paper, wear a linen shirt, cross the ocean in a clipper-ship, and burn wood in an open fire-place, something might be done.

As Picton's steamer (probably fog-bound) had not yet arrived in Sydney, nor yet indeed the "Balaklava," the traveller determined to take a Newfoundland brigantine for St. John's, from which port there are vessels to all parts of the world. After leaving horse and jumper with the inn-keeper, we took a small boat to one of the many queer looking, high-pooped crafts in the harbor, and very soon found ourselves in a tiny cabin, panelled with maple, in which the captain and some of the men were busy over a pan of savory *lobscouse*, a salt-sea dish of great reputation and flavor. Picton soon made his agreement with the captain for a four days' sail (or more) across to the neighboring province, and his luggage was to be on board the next morning. Once more we sailed over the bay of Sydney, and regained the pleasant shelter of our inn.

"Picton," said I, after a comfortable supper and a pensive segar, "we shall soon separate for our respective homes; but before we part, I wish to say to you how much I have enjoyed this brief acquaintance; perhaps we may never meet again, but I trust our short voyage together, will now and then be recalled by you, in whatever part of the world you may chance to be, as it certainly will by me."

The traveller replied by a hearty, earnest grasp of the hand; and then, after this formal leave-taking, we became suddenly estranged, as it were, sad, and silent, and shy; the familiar tone of conversation lost its key-note; Picton looked out of the inn window at the luminous moon-fog on the bay, and I buried my reflections in an antiquated pamphlet of "Household Words." We were soon interrupted by a stranger coming into the parlor, a chance visitor, another dry, preceese specimen of the land of oat-cakes.

After the usual salutations, the conversation floated easily on, upon indifferent topics, until Picton happened to allude, casually, to the general banking system of England. This was enough for a text. Our visitor immediately launched forth upon the subject, and gaed us a twa-hours discourse on the system of banking in Scotland; wherein the superiority of the method adopted by his countrymen, to wring the last drop of interest out a shilling, was pertinaciously and dogmatically argued, upon the great groundwork of "the general and aibstract preencepels of feenance!"

It was in vain that the traveller endeavored to silence him by a few flashes of sarcasm. He might as well have tried to silence a park of artillery with a handful of torpedoes! On and on, with the doggedness of a slow-hound, the Scot pursued the theme, until all other considerations were lost in the one sole idea.

But thus it is always, when you come in contact with people of "aibstract preencepels." All sweet and tender impulses, all generous and noble suggestions, all light and shade, all warmth and color, must give place to these dry husks of reason.

"Confound the Scotch interloper," said Picton, after our visitor had retired, "what business had he to impose upon our good nature, with his threadbare 'aibstract preencepels?' Confound him and his beggarly high cheek-bones, and his Caledonian pock-pits. I am sorry that I ever came to this part of the world; it has ruined a taste which I had acquired, with much labor, for Scottish poetry; and I shall never see 'Burns's Works' again without a sickening shudder."

CHAPTER XI.

The Bras d'Or Road—Farewell to Picton—Home sweet Home—The Rob Roys of Cape Breton—Note and Query—Chapel Island—St. Peter's—Enterprise—The Strait of Canseau—West River—The last Out-post of the Scottish Chiefs.

The road that skirts the Arm of Gold is about one hundred miles in length. After leaving Sydney, you ride beside the Spanish River a short distance, until you come to the portage, which separates it from the lake, and then you follow the delicious curve of the great beach until you arrive at St. Peter's. From St. Peter's you travel across a narrow strip of land until you reach the shore upon the extreme westerly end of the island of Cape Breton, where you cross the Strait of Canseau, and then you are upon the mainland of Nova Scotia. I had fondly hoped to voyage upon the Bras d'Or, instead of beside it; but was obliged to forego that pleasure. Romance, at one dollar per mile, is a dear piece of extravagance, even in so ethereal a vehicle as a birch-bark canoe. Therefore I engaged a seat in the Cape Breton stage, instead of the aboriginal conveyance, in which you have to sit or lie in the bottom, at the risk of an upset, and trust to fair weather and the dip of the paddle.

At day-break (two o'clock in the morning in these high latitudes) the stage drove up to the door of our pleasant inn. I was speedily dressed, and ready—and now—"Good bye, Picton!"

The traveller stretched out a hand from the warm nest in which he was buried.

"Good bye," he said, with a hearty hand-shake, and so we parted.

It was painful to leave such an agreeable companion, but then what a relief it was to escape from the cannie Scots! The first inhalation of the foggy air went tingling through every vein; the first movement of the stage, as we rolled westward, was indescribable happiness; I was at last homeward bound; in full health, in full strength; swift upon my sight came the vision of the one familiar river; the cottage and the chestnuts; the rolling greensward, and the Palisades; and there, too, was my best friend; and there—

"My young barbarians all at play."

Drive on, John Ormond!

Our Cape Breton stage is an easy, two-seated vehicle; a quiet, little rockaway-wagon, with a top; and although H. B. M. Royal Mail Coach, entirely different from the huge musk-melon upon wheels with which we are familiar in the States. In it I am the only passenger. Thank Heaven for that! I might be riding beside an aibstract preencepel.

But never mind! Drive on, John Ormond; we shall soon be among another race of Scotsmen, the bold Highlandmen of romance; the McGregors, and McPhersons, the Camerons, Grahams, and McDonalds; and as a century or so does not alter the old-country prejudices of the people in these settlements, we will no doubt find them in their pristine habiliments; in plaids and spleuchens; brogues and buckles; hose and bonnets; with claymore, dirk, and target; the white cockade and eagle feather, so beautiful in the Waverley Novels.

We left the pretty village of Sydney behind us, and were not long in gaining the margin of the Bras d'Or. This great lake, or rather arm of the sea, is, as I have said, about one hundred miles in length by its shore road; but so wide is it, and so indented by broad bays and deep coves, that a coasting journey around it is equal in extent to a voyage across the Atlantic. Besides the distant mountains that rise proudly from the remote shores, there are many noble islands in its expanse, and forest-covered peninsulas, bordered with beaches of glittering white pebbles. But over all this wide landscape there broods a spirit of primeval solitude; not a sail broke the loneliness of the lake until we had advanced far upon our day's journey. For strange as it may seem, the Golden Arm is a very useless piece of water in this part of the world; highly favored as it is by nature, land-locked, deep enough for vessels of all burden, easy of access on the gulf side, free from fogs, and only separated from the ocean at its western end by a narrow strip of land, about three quarters of a mile wide; abounding in timber, coal, and gypsum, and valuable for its fisheries, especially in winter, yet the Bras d'Or is undeveloped for want of that element which scorns to be alien to the Colonies, namely, enterprise.

If I had formed some romantic ideas concerning the new and strange people we found on the road we were now travelling, the Highlandmen, the Rob Roys and Vich Ian Vohrs of Nova Scotia, those ideas were soon dissipated. It is true here were the Celts in their wild settlements, but without bagpipes or pistols, sporrans or philabegs; there was not even a solitary thistle to charm the eye; and as for oats, there were at least two Scotchmen to one oat in this garden of exotics. I have a reasonable amount of respect for a Highlandman in full costume; but for a carrot-headed, freckled, high-cheeked animal, in a round hat and breeches, that cannot utter a word of English, I have no sympathy. One fellow of this complexion, without a hat, trotted beside our coach for several miles, grunting forth his infernal Gaelic to John Ormond, with a hah! to every answer of the driver, that was really painful. When he disappeared in the woods his red head went out like a torch. But we had scarcely gone by the first Highlandman, when another darted out upon us from a by-path, and again broke the sabbath of the woods and waters; and then another followed, so that the morning ride by the Bras d'Or was fringed with Gaelic. Now I have heard many languages in my time, and know how to appreciate the luxurious Greek, the stately Latin, the mellifluous Chinese, the epithetical Sclavic, the soft Italian, the rich Castilian, the sprightly French, sonorous German, and good old English, but candor compels me to say, that I do not think much of the Gaelic. It is not pleasing to the ear.

Yet it was a stately ride, that by the Bras d'Or; in one's own coach, as it were, traversing such old historic ground. For the very name, and its associations, carry one back to the earliest discoveries in America, carry one back behind Plymouth Rock to the earlier French adventurers in this hemisphere; yea, almost to the times of Richard Crookback; for on the neighboring shores, as the English claim, Cabot first landed, and named the place *Prima Vista*, in the days of Henry the Seventh, the "Richmond" of history and tragedy.

"Le Bras d'Or! John Ormond, do you not think le Bras d'Or sounds much like Labrador?"

"'Deed does it," answered John.

"And why not? That mysterious, geological coast is only four days' sail from Sydney, I take it? Labrador! with its auks and puffins, its seals and sea-tigers, its whales and walruses? Why not an offshoot of le Bras d'Or, its earlier brother in the family of discovery. But drive on, John Ormond, we will leave etymology to the pedants."

Well, well, ancient or modern, there is not a lovelier ride by white-pebbled beach and wide stretch of wave. Now we roll along amidst primeval trees, not the evergreens of the sea-coast, but familiar growths of maple, beech, birch; and larches, juniper or hackmatack—imperishable for ship craft. Now we cross bridges, over sparkling brooks, alive with trout and salmon, and most surprising of all, pregnant with water-power. "Surprising," because no motive-power can be presented to the eye of a citizen of the young republic without the corresponding thought of "Why not use it?" And why not, when Bras d'Or is so near, or the sea-coast either, and land at forty cents an acre, and trees as closely set, and as lofty, as ever nature planted them? Of a certainty, there would be a thousand saw-mills screaming between this and Canseau if a drop of Yankee blood had ever fertilized this soil.

Well, well, perhaps it is well. But yet to ride through a hundred miles of denationalized, high-cheeked, red, or black-headed Highlandmen, with illustrious names, in breeches and round hats, without pistols or feathers, is a sorry sight. Not one of these McGregors can earn more than five shillings a day, currency, as a laborer. Not a digger upon our canals but can do better than that; and with the chance of *rising*. But here there seems be no such opportunity. The colonial system provides that every settler shall have a grant of about one hundred and twenty acres, in fee, and free. What then? the Government fosters and protects him. It sends out annually choice stocks of cattle, at a nominal price; it establishes a tariff of duties on foreign goods, so low that the revenue derived therefrom is not sufficient to pay the salaries of its officers. What then? The colonist is only a parasite with all these advantages. He is not an integral part of a nation; a citizen, responsible for his franchise. He is but a colonial Micmac, or Scotch-Mac; a mere sub-thoughted, irresponsible exotic, in a governmental cold grapery. By the great forefinger of Tom Jefferson, I would rather be a citizen of the United States than *own* all the five-shilling Blue Noses between Sydney and Canseau!

As we roll along up hill and down, a startling flash of sunlight bursts forth from the dewy morning clouds, and touches lake, island, and promontory, with inexpressible beauty. Stop, John Ormond, or drive slowly; let us enjoy *dolce far niente*. To hang now in our curricle upon this wooded hill-top, overlooking the clear surface of the lake, with leafy island, and peninsula dotted in its depths, in all its native grace, without a touch or trace of handwork, far or near, save and except a single spot of sail in the far-off, is holy and sublime.

And there we rested, reverentially impressed with the week-day sabbath. We lingered long and lovingly upon our woody promontory, our eyrie among the spruces of Cape Breton.

"Clear, placid Leman! thy contrasted lake,With the wild world I dwelt in, is a thingWhich warns me, with its stillness, to forsakeEarth's troubled waters for a purer spring."

Down hill go horses and mail-coach, and we are lost in a vast avenue of twinkling birches. For miles we ride within breast-high hedges of sunny shrubs, until we reach another promontory, where Bras d'Or again breaks forth, with bay, island, white beach, peninsula, and sparkling cove. And before us, bowered in trees, lies Chapel Island, the Micmac Mecca, with its Catholic Church and consecrated ground. Here at certain seasons the red men come to worship the white Christ. Here the western descendants of Ishmael pitch their bark tents, and swing their barbaric censers before the Asiatic-born Redeemer. "They that dwell in the wilderness shall bow before Him." That gathering must be a touching sermon to the heart of faith!

But we roll onwards, and now are again on the clearings, among the log-cabins of the Highlandmen. Although every settler has his governmental farm, yet nearly the whole of it is still in forest-land. A log hut and cleared-acre lot, with Flora McIvor's grubbing, hoeing, or chopping, while their idle lords and masters trot beside the mail-coach to hear the news, are the only results of the home patronage. At last we come to a gentle declivity, a bridge lies below us, a wider brook; we cross over to find a cosy inn and a rosy landlord on the other side; and John Ormond lays down the ribbons, after a sixty-mile drive, to say: "This is St. Peter's."

Now so far us the old-fashioned inns of New Scotland are concerned, I must say they make me ashamed of our own. Soap, sand, and water, do not cost so much as carpets, curtains, and fly-blown mirrors; but still, to the jaded traveller, they have a more attractive aspect. We sit before a snow-white table without a cloth, in the inn-parlor, kitchen, laundry, and dining-room, all in one, just over against the end of the lake; and enjoy a rasher of bacon and eggs with as much gusto as if we were in the midst of a palace of fresco. Ornamental eating has become with us a species of gaudy, ostentatious vulgarity; and a dining-room a sort of fool's paradise. I never think of the little simple meal at St. Peter's now, without tenderness and respect.

Here we change—driver, stage, and horses. Still no other passenger. The new whip is a Yankee from the State of Maine; a tall, black-eyed, taciturn fellow, with gold rings in his ears. Now we pass the narrow strip of land that divides Bras d'Or from the ocean. It is only three-quarters of a mile wide between water and water, and look at Enterprise digging out a canal! By the bronze statue of De Witt Clinton, if there are not three of the five-shilling Rob Roys at work, with two shovels, a horse, and one cart!

As we approach Canseau the landscape becomes flat and uninteresting; but distant ranges of mountains rise up against the evening sky, and as we travel on towards their bases they attract the eye more and more. Ear-rings is not very communicative. He does not know the names of any of them. Does not know how high they are, but has heard say they are the highest mountains in Nova Scotia. "Are those the mountains of Canseau?" Yes, them's them. So with renewed anticipations we ride on towards the strait "of unrivalled beauty," that travellers say "surpasses anything in America."

And, indeed, Canseau can have my feeble testimony in confirmation. It is a grand marine highway, having steep hills on the Cape Breton Island side, and lofty mountains on the other shore; a full, broad, mile-wide space between them; and reaching from end to end, fifteen miles, from the Atlantic to the Gulf of St. Lawrence. As I took leave of Ear-rings, at Plaister Cove, and wrapped myself up in my cloak in the stern-sheets of the row-boat to cross the strait, the full Acadian moon, larger than any United States moon, rose out of her sea-fog, and touched mountain, height, and billow, with effulgence. It was a scene of Miltonic grandeur. After the ruined walls of Louisburgh, and the dark caverns of Sydney, comes Canseau, with its startling splendors! Truly this is a wonderful country.

Another night in a clean Nova-Scotian inn on the mountain-side, a deep sleep, and balmy awakening in the clear air. Yet some exceptions must be taken to the early sun in this latitude. To get up at two o'clock or four; to ride thirty or forty miles to breakfast, with a convalescent appetite, is painful. But yet, "to him, who in the love of Nature holds communion with her visible forms, she speaks a various language." Admiration and convalescent hunger make a very good team in this beautiful country. You look out upon the unfathomable Gulf of St. Lawrence, and feel as if you were an unfathomable gulf yourself. You ride through lofty woods, with a tantalizing profusion of living edibles in your path; at every moment a cock-rabbit is saying his prayers before the horses; at every bosk and bole a squirrel stares at you with unwinking eyes, and Robin Yellow-bill hops, runs, and flies before the coach within reach of the driver's whip, *sans peur!* And this too is the land of moose and cariboo: here the hunters, on snow-shoes, track the huge animals in the season; and moose and cariboo, in the Halifax markets, are cheaper than beef with us. And to think this place is only a four days' journey from the metropolis, in the languid winter! By the ashes of Nimrod, I will launch myself on a pair of snow-shoes, and shoot a moose in the snow before I am twelve months older, as sure as these ponies carry us to breakfast!

"How far are we from breakfast, driver?"

"Twenty miles," quoth Jehu.

Now I had been anxious to get a sight of our ponies, for the sake of estimating their speed and endurance; but at this time they were not in sight. For the coach we (three passengers) were in, was built like an omnibus-sleigh on wheels, with a high seat and "dasher" in front, so that we could not see what it was that drew our ark, and therefore I climbed up in the driver's perch to overlook our motors. There were four of them; little, shaggy, black ponies, with bunchy manes and fetlocks, not much larger than Newfoundland dogs. Yet they swept us along the road as rapidly as if they were full-sized horses, up hill and down, without visible signs of fatigue.

And now we passed through another French settlement, "Tracadie," and again the Norman kirtle and petticoat of the pastoral, black-eyed Evangelines hove in sight, and passed like a day-dream. And here we are in an English settlement, where we enjoy a substantial breakfast, and then again ride through the primeval woods, with an occasional glimpse of the broad Gulf and its mountain scenery, until we come upon a pretty inland village, by name Antigonish.

At Antigonish, we find a bridal party, and thepretty English landlady offers us wine and cake with hospitable welcome; and a jovial time of it we have until we are summoned, by crack of whip, to ride over to West River.

I must say that the natural prejudices we have against Nova Scotia are ill-placed, unjust, and groundless. The country itself is the great redeeming feature of the province, and a very large portion of it is uninfested by Scotchmen. Take for instance the road we are now travelling. For hours we bowl along a smooth turnpike, in the midst of a deep forest: although scarce a week has elapsed since these gigantic trees were leafless, yet the foliage has sprung forth as it were with a touch, and now the canopy of leaves about us, and overhead, is so dense as scarcely to afford a twinkle of light from the sun. Sometimes we ride by startling precipices and winding streams; sometimes overlook an English settlement, with its rolling pasture-lands, bare of trees and rich in verdure. At last we approach the precincts of Northumberland Strait, and are cleverly carried into New Glasgow. It is fast-day, and the shops are closed in Sabbath stillness; but on the sign-boards of the village one reads the historic names of "Ross" and "Cameron;" and

"Graham," "McGregor" and "McDonald." What a pleasant thing it must be to live in that village! Here too I saw for the first time in the province a thistle! But it was a silver-plated one, in the blue bonnet of a "pothecary's boy." A metallic effigy of the original plant, that had bloomed some generations ago in native land. There was poetry in it, however, even on the brow of an incipient apothecary.

When we had put New Glasgow behind us, we felt relieved, and rode along the marshes on the border of the strait that divides the Province from Prince Edward's Island, so named in honor of his graceless highness the Duke of Kent, Edward, father of our Queen Victoria. Thence we came forth upon higher ground, the coal-mines of Pictou; and here is the great Pictou railway, from the mines to the town, six miles in length. Then by rolling hill and dale down to West River, where John Frazer keeps the Twelve-Mile House. This inn is clean and commodious; only twelve miles from Pictou; and, reader, I would advise you, as twelve miles is but a short distance, to go to Pictou without stopping at West River. For John Frazer's is a house of petty annoyances. From the moment you enter, you feel the insolence of the surly, snarling landlord, and his no less gifted lady; the same old greed which has no eye except for money; the miserly table, for which you are obliged to pay before hand; the lack of attendance; the abundance of impertinence. Just as you are getting into bed you are peremptorily called to the door to pay for your room, which haply you had forgotten; if you want your boots brushed the answer is, "Perhaps"—if you request them to call you in the morning, for the only stage, they say, "Just as it happens;" (indeed, it was only by accident that the stage-driver discovered he had one more trunk than his complement of passengers, and so awoke me just as the coach was on the point of departure;) if you can submit to all this, then, reader, go to Twelve-Mile House, at West River.

We left this last outpost of the Scotch settlements with pleasure. After all, there is a secret feeling of joy in contrasting one's self with such wretched, penurious, mis-made specimens of the human animal. And from this time henceforth I shall learn to prize my own language, and not be carried away by any catch-penny Scotch synonyms, such as the *lift* for the sky, and the *gloamin* for twilight. And as for *poortith cauld*, and *pauky chiel*, I leave them to those who can appreciate them:

"Farewell, farewell, beggarly Scotland,Cold and beggarly poor countrie;If ever I cross thy border again,The muckle deil maun carry me."

CHAPTER XII.

The Ride from West River—A Fellow Passenger—Parallels of History—One Hundred Romances—Baron de Castine—His Character—Made Chief of the Abenaquis—Duke of York's Charter—Encroachments of the Puritans—Church's Indian Wars—False Reports—Reflections.

It would make a curious collection of pictures if I had obtained photographs of all the coaches I travelled in, and upon, during my brief sojourn in the province; some high, some low, some red, some green, or yellow as it chanced, with horses few or many, often superior animals—stylish, fast, and sound; and again, the most diminutive of ponies, such as Monsieur the Clown drives into the ring of his canvass coliseum when he utters the pleasant salute of "Here I am, with all my little family?" This morning we have the old, familiar stage-coach of Yankee land—red, picked out with yellow; high, narrow, iron steps; broad thoroughbraces; wide seats; all jingle, tip, tilt, and rock, from one end of the road to the other. My fellow traveller on the box is a little man with a big hat; soft spoken, sweet voiced, and excessively shy and modest. But this was a most pleasing change from the experiences of the last few hours, let me tell you; and, if you ever travel by West River, you will find any change pleasant—no matter what.

My companion was shy, but not taciturn; on the contrary, he could talk well enough after the ice was broken, and long enough, too, for that matter. I found that he was a Church of England clergyman by profession, and a Welshman by birth. He was well versed in the earlier history of the colony—that portion of it which

171

is by far the most interesting—I mean its French or Acadian period. "There are in the traditions and scattered fragments of history that yet survive in this once unhappy land," he said, in a peculiarly low and mellifluous voice, "much that deserves to be embalmed in story and in poetry. Your Longfellow has already preserved one of the most touching of its incidents; but I think I am safe in asserting that there yet remain the materials of one hundred romances. Take the whole history of Acadia during the seventeenth century—the almost patriarchal simplicity of its society, the kindness, the innocence, the virtues of its people; the universal toleration which prevailed among them, in spite of the interference of the home government; look," said he, "at the perfect and abiding faith which existed between them and the Indians! Does the world-renowned story of William Penn alone merit our encomiums, except that we have forgotten this earlier but not less beautiful example? And with the true spirit of Christianity, when they refused to take up arms in their own defence, preferring rather to die by their faith than shed the blood of other men; to what parallel in history can we turn, if not to the martyred Hussites, for whom humanity has not yet dried all its tears?"

As he said this, a little flush passed over his face, and he appeared for a moment as if surprised at his own enthusiasm; then shrinking under his big hat again, he relapsed into silence.

We rode on for some time without a word on either side, until I ventured to remark that I coincided with him in the belief that Acadia was the romantic ground of early discovery in America; and that even the fluent pen of Hawthorne had failed to lend a charm to the harsh, repulsive, acrimonious features of New England's colonial history.

"I have read but one book of Hawthorne's," said he—"'The Scarlet Letter.' I do not coincide with you; I think that to be a remarkable instance of the triumph of genius over difficulties. By the way," said he, "speaking of authors, what an exquisite poem Tom Moore would have written, had he visited Chapel Island, which you have seen no doubt? (here he gave a little nod with the big hat) and what a rich volume would have dropped from the arabesque pen of your own Irving (another nod), had he written the life of the Baron de St. Castine, chief of the Abenaquis, as he did that of Philip of Pokanoket."

"Do you know the particulars of that history?" said I.

"I do not know the particulars," he replied, "only the outlines derived from chronicle and tradition. Imagination," he added, with a faint smile, "can supply the rest, just as an engineer pacing a bastion can draw from it the proportions of the rest of the fortress."

And then, from under the shelter of the big hat, there came low and sad tones of music, like a requiem over a bier, upon which are laid funeral flowers, and sword, and plume; a melancholy voice almost intoning the history of a Christian hero, who had been the chief of that powerful nation—the rightful owners of the fair lands around us. Even if memory could now supply the words, it would fail to reproduce the effect conveyed by the tones of *that voice*. And of the story itself I can but furnish the faint outlines:

FAINT OUTLINES.

Baron de St. Castine, chief of the Abenaquis, was a Frenchman, born in the little village of Oberon, in the province of Bearn, about the middle of the seventeenth century. Three great influences conspired to make him unhappy—first, education, which at that time was held to be a reputable part of the discipline of the scions of noble families; next, a delicate and impressible mind, and lastly, he was born under the shadow of the Pyrenees, and within sight of the Atlantic. He had also served in the wars of Louis XIV. as colonel of the Carrignan, Cavignon, or Corignon regiment; therefore, from his military education, was formed to endure, or to think lightly of hardships. Although not by profession a Protestant, yet he was a liberal Catholic. The doctrines of Calvin had been spread throughout the province during his youth, and John la Placette, a native of Bearn, was then one of the leaders of the free churches of Copenhagen, in Denmark, and of Utrecht, in Holland.

But, whatever his religious prejudices may have been, they do not intrude themselves in any part of his career; we know him only as a pure Christian, an upright man, and a faithful friend of humanity. Like many other Frenchmen of birth and education in those days, the Baron de St. Castine had been attracted by descriptions of newly discovered countries in the western hemisphere, and fascinated by the ideal life of the children of nature. To a mind at once susceptible and heroic, impulsive by temperament, and disciplined to endure, such promptings have a charm that is irresistible. As the chronicler relates, he preferred the forests of Acadia, to the Pyrenian mountains that compassed the place of his nativity, and taking up his abode with the savages, on the first year behaved himself so among them as to draw from them their inexpressible esteem. He married a woman of the nation, and repudiating their example, did not change his wife, by which he taught his wild neighbors that God did not love inconstancy. By this woman, his first and only wife, he had one son and two daughters, the latter were afterwards married, "very handsomely, to Frenchmen, and had good dowries." Of the son there is preserved a single touching incident. In person the baron was strikingly handsome, a fine form, a well featured face, with a noble expression of candor, firmness and benevolence. Possessed of an ample fortune, he used it to enlarge the comforts of the people of his adoption; these making him a recompense in beaver skins and other rich furs, from which he drew a still larger revenue, to be in turn again devoted to the objects of his benevolence. It was said of him, "that he can draw from his coffers two or three hundred thousand crowns of good dry gold; but all the use he makes of it is to buy presents for his *fellow savages*, who, upon their return from hunting, present him with skins to treble the value."

Is it then surprising that this man, so wise, so good, so faithful to his *fellow savages*, should, after twenty years, rise to the most eminent station in that unsophisticated nation? That indeed these simple Indians, who knew no arts except those of peace and war, should have looked up to him as their tutular god? By the treaty of Breda, the lands from the Penobscots to Nova Scotia had been ceded to France, in exchange for the island of St. Christopher. Upon these lands the Baron de St. Castine had peacefully resided for many years, until a new patent was granted to the Duke of

York, the boundaries of which extended beyond the limits of the lands ceded by the treaty. Oh, those patents! those patents! What wrongs were perpetrated by those remorseless instruments; what evil councils prevailed when they were hatched; what corrupt, what base, what knavish hands formed them; what vile, what ignoble, what ponderous lies has history assumed to maintain, or to excuse them, and the acts committed under them?

The first English aggression after the treaty, was but a trifling one in respect to immediate effects. A quantity of wine having been landed by a French vessel upon the lands covered by the patent, was seized by the Duke of York's agents. This, upon a proper representation by the French ambassador at the court of Charles II., was restored to the rightful owners. But thereupon a new boundary line was run, *and the whole of Castine's plantations included within it.* Immediately after this, the Rose frigate, under the command of Captain Andross, sailed up the Penobscot, plundered and destroyed Castine's house and fort, and sailed away with all his arms and goods. Not only this, intruders from other quarters invaded the lands of the Indians, took possession of the rivers, and spoiled the fisheries with seines, turned their cattle in to devour the standing corn of the Abenaquis, and committed other depredations, which, although complained of, were neither inquired into nor redressed.

Then came reprisals; and first the savages retaliated by killing the cattle of their enemies. Then followed those fearful and bloody campaigns, which, under the name of Church's Indian Wars, disgrace the early annals of New England. Night surprises, butcheries that spared neither age nor sex, prisoners taken and sold abroad into slavery, after the glut of revenge was satiated, these to return and bring with them an inextinguishable hatred against the English, and desire of revenge. Anon a conspiracy and the surprisal of Dover, accompanied with all the appalling features of barbaric warfare—Major Waldron being tied down by the Indians in his own arm-chair, and each one of them drawing a sharp knife across his breast, says with the stroke, "Thus I cross out my account;" these, and other atrocities, on either side, constitute the principal records of a Christian people, who professed to be only pilgrims and sojourners in a strange land—the victims of persecution in their own.

During all this dark and bloody period, no name is more conspicuous in the annals than that of the Chief of the Abenaquis. Like a frightful ogre, he hovers in the background, deadly and ubiquitous—the terror of the colonies. It was he who had stirred up the Indians to do the work. Then come reports of a massacre in some town on the frontier, and with it is coupled a whisper of "Castine!" a fort has been surprised, he is there! Some of Church's men have fallen in an ambuscade; the baron has planned it, and furnished the arms and ammunition by which the deed was consummated! Superstition invests him with imaginary powers; fanaticism exclaims, 'tis he who had taught the savages to believe that we are the people who crucified the Saviour.

But in spite of all these stories, the wonderful Bernese is not captured, nor indeed seen by any, except that sometimes an English prisoner escaping from the enemy, comes to tell of his clemency and tenderness; he has bound up the wounds of these, he has saved the lives of those. At last a small settlement of French

177

and Indians is attacked by Church's men at Penobscot, every person there being either killed or taken prisoner; among the latter a daughter of the great baron, with her children, from whom they learn that her unhappy father, ruined and broken-hearted, had returned to France, the victim of persecutors, who, under the name of saints, exhibited a cruelty and rapacity that would have disgraced the reputation of a Philip or an Alva!

"It is a matter of surprise to the historical student," said the little man, "that with a people like yours, so conspicuous in many rare examples of erudition, that the history of Acadia has not merited a closer attention, throwing as it does so strong a reflective light upon your own. Such a task doubtless does not present many inviting features, especially to those who would preserve, at any sacrifice of truth, the earlier pages of discovery in America, pure, spotless, and unsullied. But I think this dark, tragic background would set off all the brighter the characters of those really good men who flourished in that period, of whom there were no doubt many, although now obscured by the dull, dead moonshine of indiscriminate forefathers' flattery. I know very well that in some regards we might copy the example of a few of the first planters of New England, but for the rest I believe with Adam Clark, that for the sake of humanity, it were better that such ages should never return."

"We talk much," says he, "of ancient manners, their *simplicity and ingenuousness*, and say that *the former days were better than these*. But who says this who is a judge of the times? In those days of celebrated simplicity, there were not so many crimes as at present, I grant; but what they wanted in *number*, they made up in *degree*, *deceit*, *cruelty*, *rapine*, *murder*, and *wrong* of almost every kind, then flourished. *We are refined* in our vices, they were *gross and barbarous* in theirs. They had neither so many *ways* nor so many *means* of sinning; but the *sum* of their moral turpitude was greater than ours. We have a sort of *decency* and good *breeding*, which lay a certain restraint on our passions; they were boorish and beastly, and their bad passions ever in full play. Civilization prevents barbarity and atrocity; mental cultivation induces decency of manners—those primitive times were generally without these. Who that knows them would wish such ages to return?"[A]

CHAPTER XIII.

Truro—On the Road to Halifax—Drive to the Left—A Member of the Foreign Legion—Irish Wit at Government Expense—The first Battle of the Legion—Ten Pounds Reward—Sir John Gaspard's Revenge—The Shubenacadie Lakes—Dartmouth Ferry, and the Hotel Waverley.

Pleasant Truro! At last we regain the territories of civility and civilization! Here is the honest little English inn, with its cheerful dining-room, its clean spread, its abundant dishes, its glass of ripe ale, its pleased alacrity of service. After our long ride from West River, we enjoy the best inn's best room, the ease, the comfort, and the fair aspect of one of the prettiest towns in the province. Truro is situated on the head waters of the Basin of Minas, or Cobequid Bay, as it is denominated on the map, between the Shubenacadie and Salmon rivers. Here we are within fifty miles of the idyllic land, the pastoral meadows of Grand-Pré! But, alas! there is yet a long ride before us; the path from Truro to Grand-Pré being in the shape of an acute angle, of which Halifax is the apex. As yet there is no direct road from place to place, but by the shores of the Basin of Minas. Let us look, however, at pleasant Truro.

One of the striking features of this part of the country is the peculiarity of the rivers; these are full or empty, with every flux and reflux of the tide; for instance, when we crossed the Salmon, we saw only a high, broad, muddy ditch, drained to the very bottom. This is owing to the ocean tides, which, sweeping up the Bay of Fundy, pour into the Basin of Minas, and fill all its tributary streams; then, with prodigal reaction, sweeping forth again, leave only the vacant channels of the rivers—if they may be called by that name. This peculiar feature of hydrography is of course local—limited to this section of the province—indeed if it be not to this corner of the world. The country surrounding the village is well cultivated, diversified with rolling hill and dale, and although I had not the opportunity of seeing much of it, yet the mere description of its natural scenery was sufficiently tempting. Here, too, I saw something that reminded me of home— a clump of cedar-trees! These of course were exotics, brought, not without expense, from the States, planted in the courtyard of a little aristocratic cottage, and protected in winter by warm over-coats of wheat straw. So we go! Here they grub up larches and spruces to plant cedars.

The mail coach was soon at the door of our inn, and after taking leave of my fellow-traveller with the big hat, I engaged a seat on the stage-box beside Jeangros, a French Canadian, or Canuck—one of the best whips on the line. Jeangros is not a great portly fellow, as his name would seem to indicate, but a spare, small man— nevertheless with an air of great courage and command. Jeangros touched up the leaders, the mail-coach rattled through the street of the town, and off we trotted from Truro into the pleasant road that leads to Halifax.

One thing I observed in the province especially worthy of imitation—the old English practice of turning to the *left* in driving, instead of to the *right*, as we do. Let me exhibit the merits of the respective systems by a brief diagram. By the English system they drive thus:

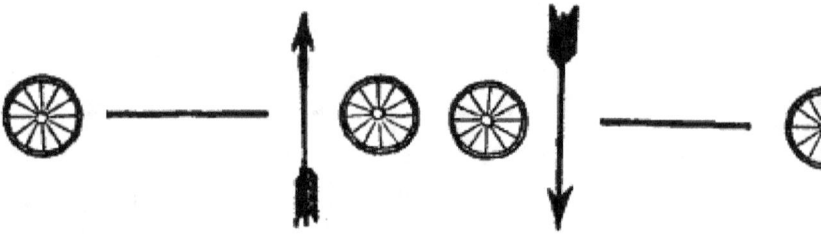

The arrows represent the drivers, as well as the directions of the vehicles; of course when two vehicles, coming in opposite directions, pass each other on the road, each driver is nearest the point of contact, and can see readily, and provide against accidents. Now contrast our system with the former:

no wonder we have so many collisions.

"The rule of the road is a paradox quite, In driving your carriage along, If you keep to the left, you are sure to go right, If you keep to the right, you go wrong."

It would be a good thing if our present senseless laws were reversed in this matter, and a few lives saved, and a few broken limbs prevented.

When I took leave of my native country for a short sojourn in this province, the great question then before the public was the invasion of international law, by the British minister and a whole solar system of British consuls. I had the pleasure of being a fellow exile on the Canada with Mr. Crampton, Mr. Barclay, and Mr. ——, Her British Majesty's representatives, and of course felt no little interest to know the fate of the *Foreign Legion*.

Before I left Halifax, I learned some particulars of that famous flock of jail birds. All that we knew, at home, was that a number of recruits for the Crimea had been picked up in the streets and alleys of Columbia, and carried, at an enormous expense, to Halifax, there to be enrolled. And also, that as a mere cover to this infraction of the law of Neutrality, the men were engaged as laborers, to work upon the public improvements of Nova Scotia. The sequel of that enterprise remained to be told. A majority of these recruits were Irishmen—some of them not wanting in the mother wit of the race. So when they were gathered in the great province building at Halifax, and Sir John Gaspard le Marchant, in chapeau, feather and sword, came down to review his levies, with great spirit and military pomp, "Well, my men," said he, "you are here to enlist, eh, and serve Her Majesty?" To which the spokesman of the Foreign Legion, fully understanding the beauty of his position, replied, with a sly twinkle of the eye, "We didn't engage to 'list at all, at all, but to wurruk on the railroad." Upon which Sir John Gaspard, seeing that Her Majesty had been imposed upon, politely told the legion to go to——Dante's Inferno.

Now whether the place to which the Foreign Legion was consigned by Sir John Gaspard, possessed even less attractions than Halifax, or from whatever reason soever, it chanced that the jolly boys, raked from our alleys and jails, never stirred a foot out of the province; and while the peace of the whole world was endangered by their abduction, as that of Greece and Troy had been by the rape of Helen, they were quietly enlisting in less warlike expeditions—in fact, engaging themselves to work upon that great railroad, of which mention has been made heretofore.

Now we have seen something of the clannish propensities of the people of the colonies, and the contractors knew what sort of material they had to deal with. And, inasmuch as there was a pretty large group of five-shilling Highlandmen, grading, levelling, and filling in one end of a section of the road, the gang of Irishmen was placed at the opposite end, as far from them as possible, which no doubt would have preserved peaceful relations between the two, but for the fact, that as the work progressed the hostile forces naturally approached each other. It was towards the close of a summer evening, that the ground was broken by the gentlemen of the shamrock, within sight of the shanties decorated with the honorable order of the thistle. A lovely evening in the month of June! Not with spumy cannon and prickly bayonets, but with peaceful spade and mattock, advanced the sons of St. Patrick towards the children of a sister isle. Then did Roderick Dhu step forth from his shanty, and inquire, in choice Gaelic, if a person named Brian Borheime was in the ranks of the approaching forces. Then then did Brian Borheime advance, spade in hand, and with a single spat of his implement level Roderick, as though he had been a piece of turf. Then was Brian flattened out by the spade of Vich Ian Vohr; and Vich Ian Vohr, by the spade of Captain Rock. Then fell Captain Rock by the spade of Rob Roy; and Rob Roy smelt the earth under the spade of Handy Andy. In a word, the fight became general—the bagpipe blew to arms—Celt joined Celt, there was the tug of war; but the sun set upon the lowered standard of the thistle, and victory proclaimed Shamrock the conqueror. Several of the natives were left for dead upon the field of battle, the triumphant Irish ran away, to a man, to avoid the consequences, and I blush to say it, as I do to record any act of heartless ingratitude, handbills were speedily posted up by the order of government, offering a reward of ten pounds apiece for the capture of certain members of the Foreign Legion, who had been the ringleaders in the riot, which handbill was not only signed by that seducer of soldiers, Sir John Gaspard le Marchant, but also ornamented with the horn of the unicorn and the claws of the British lion.

But there is a Nemesis even in Nova Scotia, for this riot produced effects, unwonted and unlooked for. One of the prominent leaders in the Nova Scotia Parliament, a gentleman distinguished both as an orator and as a poet—the Hon. Joseph Howe, who had signalized himself as an advocate of the right of Her Majesty to recruit for the Crimea in the streets of Columbia, and was ready to pit the British Lion against the American Eagle in support of that right, fell by the very legion he had been so zealous to create. The Hon. Joseph Howe, M. P., by the support of the Irish population, could always command a *popular* majority and keep his seat in the house, so long as he maintained his loyalty to this votive class of citizens. But, unfortunately, Hon. Joseph Howe, in alluding to the riot, took the Scotch side of the broil. This was sufficient. At the election following he was a defeated candidate, and politely advised to retire to private life. Thus was the Hon. J. H. "hoist by his own petard," the first man to fall by this expensive military company.

An adventure upon the Shubenacadie brought one of these heroes into prominent relief. After we had parted from pleasant Truro, at every nook and corner of the road, there seemed to be a passenger waiting for the Halifax coach. So that the top of the vehicle was soon filled with dusty fellow-travellers, and Jeangros was getting to be a little impatient. Just as we turned into the densest part of the forest, where the evening sun was most obscured by the close foliage, we saw two men, one decorated with a pair of handcuffs, and the other armed with a brace of pistols. The latter hailed the coach.

"What d'ye want?" quoth Jeangros, drawing up by the roadside.

"Government prisoner," said the man with the pistols.

"What the —— is government prisoner to me?" quoth Jeangros.

"I want to take him to Dartmouth," said the tall policeman.

"Then take him there," said our jolly driver, shaking up the leaders.

"Hold up," shouted out the tall policeman, "I will pay his fare."

"Why didn't you say so, then?" replied Jeangros, full of the dignity of his position as driver of H. B. M. Mail-coach, before whose tin horn everything must get out of the way.

There was a doubt which was the drunkenest, the officer or the prisoner. We found out afterwards that the officer had conciliated his captive with drink, partly to keep him friendly in case of an attempted rescue, and partly to get him in such a state that running away would be impracticable. And, indeed, there would have been a great race if the prisoner had attempted to escape. The prisoner too drunk to run—the officer too drunk to pursue.

The pair had scarcely crawled up among the luggage upon the stage-top, before there was an outcry from the passengers on the box in front—"Uncock your pistols! uncock your pistols!" for the officer had dropped his fire-arms, cocked and capped, upon the top of our coach, with the muzzles pointed towards us. And indeed I may affirm here, that I never saw metallic cylinders with more menacing aspect, than those which lay quietly behind us, ready to explode—unconscious instruments as they were—and carry any of the party into the next world upon the slightest lurch of the stage-coach.

"Uncock your pistols," said the passengers.

But the officer, in the mellifluous dialect of his mother country, replied that "He'd be —— if he would. Me prishner," said he, "me prishner might escape; or, the divil knows but there might be a rescue come to him, for there's a good many of the same hereabouts."

It struck me that no person upon the top of the stage-coach was so particularly interested in this dispute as the member of the Foreign Legion, who was on his way either to the gallows or a perpetual prison. I observed that he nervously twitched at his handcuffs, perhaps—as I thought—to prepare for escape in case of an explosion; or else to be ready for the rescue; or else to take advantage of his captor, the tall policeman—jump from the stage, and run for dear life and liberty. Never was I more mistaken. True to his race, and to tradition, Pat was only striving to free himself from the leather shackles, in order to fight any man who was an enemy to his friend the policeman, and the pistols, that were cocked to shoot himself. But had not poor Paddy made such blunders in all times? The hubbub increased, a terrific contest was impending; the travellers below poked their heads out of the windows; there was every prospect of a catastrophe of some kind, when suddenly Jeangros rose to his feet, and said, in a voice clear and sharp through the tumult as an electric flash through a storm, "Uncock those pistols, or I will throw you from the top of the coach!"

There was a pause instantly, and we heard the sharp click of the cocks, as they were lowered in obedience to the little stage-driver. It had a wonderful power of command, that voice—soft and clear, but brief, decisive, authoritative.

It is quite interesting to ride fellow-passenger with a person who has played a part in the national drama, but more villainous face I never saw. Mr. Crampton, with whom I sailed on the Canada, had a much more amiable expression; indeed I think we should all be obliged to him for ridding us of at least a portion of his fellow-countrymen.

But now we ride by the Shubenacadie lakes, a chain—a bracelet—binding the province from the Basin of Minas to the seaboard. The eye never tires of this lovely feature of Acadia. Lake above lake—the division, the isthmus between, not wider than the breadth of your India shawl, my lady! I must declare that, all in all, the scenery of the province is surpassingly beautiful. As you ride by these sparkling waters, through the flowery, bowery, woods, you feel as if you like to pitch tent here—at least for the summer.

And now we approach a rustic inn by the roadside, rich in shrubbery before it, and green moss from ridge-pole to low drooping eaves, where we change horses. And as we rest here upon the wooden inn-porch, dismounted from our high perch on the stage-coach, we see right above us against the clear evening sky, Her Majesty's *ci-devant* partisan, now prisoner—by merit raised to that bad eminence. The officer hands him a glass of brandy, to keep up his spirits. The prisoner takes it, and, lifting the glass high in air, shouts out with the exultation of a fiend:

"Here's to the hinges of liberty—may they never want oil, Nor an Orangeman's bones in a pot for to boil."

Once more upon the stage to Dartmouth, where we deposit our precious fellow-travellers, and then to the ferry, and look you! across the harbor, the twinkling lights of dear old mouldy Halifax. And now we are crossing Chebucto, and the cab carries us again to our former quarters in the Hotel Waverley.

CHAPTER XIV.

Halifax again—Hotel Waverley—"Gone the Old Familiar Faces"—The Story of Marie de la Tour.

Again in old quarters! It is strange how we become attached to a place, be it what it may, if we only have known it before. The same old room we occupied years ago, however comfortless then, has a familiar air of welcome now. There is surely some little trace of self, some unseen spider-thread of attachment clinging to the walls, the old chair, the forlorn wash-stand, and the knobby four-poster, that holds the hardest of beds, the most consumptive of pillows, and a bolster as round, as white, and as hard, as a cathedral mass-candle. Heigho, Hotel Waverley! Here am I again; but where are the familiar faces? Where the brave soldier of Inkerman and Balaklava? Where the jolly old Captain of the native rifles? Where the Colonel, with his little meerschaum pipe he was so intent upon coloring? Where the party of salmon-fishermen, the Solomons of piscatology? Where the passengers by the "Canada?" And where is Picton? Gone, like last year's birds!

"A glass of ale, Henry, and one cigar, only one; I wish to be solitary."

I like this bed-room of mine at the Waverley, with its blue and white striped curtain at the window, through which the gas-lights of Halifax streets appear in lucid spots, as I wait for Henry, with the candles. Now I am no longer alone. I shut my chamber door, as it were, upon one world, only that I may enjoy another. So I trim the candles, and spread out the writing materials, and at once the characters of two centuries ago awake, and their life to me is as the life of to-day.

There is nothing more captivating in literature, than the narrative of some heroic deed of woman. Very few such are recorded; how many might be, if the actors themselves had not shunned notoriety, and "uncommended died," rather than encounter the ordeal of public praise? Of such the poet has written:

"Full many a flower is born to blush unseen, And waste its sweetness on the desert air."

Of such, many have lived and died, to live again only in fiction; whereas their own true histories would have been greater than the inventions of authors. We read of heroes laden with the "glittering spoils of empire," but the heroic deeds of woman are oftentimes, all in all, as great, without the glitter; without the pomp and pageantry of triumphal processions; without the pealing trumpet of renown. Boadicea, chained to the car of Suetonius, is the too common memorial of heroic womanity.

The story I relate is but a transcript, a mere episode in the sad history of Acadia: yet the record will be pleasing to those who estimate the merits of brave women. This, then, is the legend of

MARIE DE LA TOUR.

In the year 1621, Sir William Alexander, afterwards Earl of Sterling,[B] a romantic poet, and favorite of King James I., was presented by that monarch with a patent to all the land known as Acadia, in the Americas. Royalty in those days made out its parchment deeds for a province, without taking the trouble to search the record office, to see if there were any prior liens upon the territory. The good old rule obtained thus—

"That they may take who have the power, And they may keep who can."

or, to quote the words of another writer—

"For the time once was here, to all be it known, That all a man sailed by or saw was his own."

It is due to Sir William Alexander to say that he gave the province the proud name which at present it enjoys, of Nova Scotia, or New Scotland, a title much more appropriate than that of "Acadia,"[C] which to us means nothing.

At this time the French Colony was slowly recovering from the effects of the Argall expedition, that eight years before had laid waste its fair possessions. Among a number of emigrants from the Loire and the Seine, two gentlemen of birth and education, La Tour by name, father and son, set out to seek their fortunes in the New World. It must be remembered that in the original patent of Acadia, given by Henry IV. to De Monts, freedom of religious opinion was one of the conditions of the grant, and therefore the fact, that both the La Tours were Huguenots, did not prevent them holding commissions under the French crown, the father having in charge a small fleet of transports then ready to sail from the harbor of Brest; the son, being the commander of a fort and garrison at Cape Sable, upon the western end of Acadia.

Affairs being in this condition, it chanced that the English and French ships set sail for the same port, at about the same time; and it so happened that Sir William Alexander's fleet running afoul of the elder La Tour's in a fog, not only captured that gallant chieftain but also his transports, munitions of war, stores, artillery, etc. etc., and sailed back with the prizes to England. I beg you to observe, my dear reader, that occurrences of this kind were common enough at this period even in times of peace, and not considered piracy either, the ocean was looked upon as a mighty chessboard, and the game was won by those who could command the greatest number of pieces.

Claude de la Tour, not as a prisoner of war, but as an enforced guest of Sir William, was carried to London; and there robbed of his goods, but treated like a gentleman; introduced at Court, although deprived of his purse and liberty, and in a word, found himself surrounded with the most hostile and hospitable conditions possible in life. It is not surprising then that with true French philosophy he should have made the best of it; gained the good will of the queen, played off a little *badinage* with the ladies of the court, and forgetting the late Lady de la Tour, asleep in the old graveyard in the city of Rochelle, essayed to wear his widower weeds with that union of grace and sentiment for which his countrymen are so celebrated. The consequence was one of her majesty's maids of honor fell in love with him; the queen encouraged the match; the king had just instituted the new order of Knights Baronet, of Nova Scotia; La Tour, now in the way of good fortune, was the first to be honored with the novel title, and at the same time placed the matrimonial ring upon the finger of the love-sick maid of honor. Indeed Charles Etienne de la Tour, commandant of the little fort at Cape Sable, had scarcely lost a father, before he had gained a step-mother.

That the French widower should have been so captivated by these marks of royal favor as to lose his discretion, in the fullness of his gratitude; and, that after receiving a grant of land from his patron, as a further incentive, he should volunteer to assist in bringing Acadia under the British Crown, and as a primary step, undertake to reduce the Fort at Cape Sable; I say, that when I state this, nobody will be surprised, except a chosen few, who cherish some old-fashioned notions, in these days more romantic than real. "Two ships of war being placed under his command," he set sail, with his guns and a Step-mother, to attack the Fort at Cape Sable. The latter was but poorly garrisoned; but then it contained a Daughter-in-law! Under such circumstances, it was plain to be seen that the contest would be continued to the last ounce of powder.

Opening the trenches before the French fort, and parading his Scotch troops in the eyes of his son, the elder La Tour attempted to capture the garrison by argument. In vain he "boasted of the reception he had met with in England, of his interest at court, and the honor of knighthood which had been conferred upon him." In vain he represented "the advantages that would result from submission," the benefits of British patronage; and paraded before the eyes of the young commander the parchment grant, the seal, the royal autograph, and the glittering title of Knight Baronet, which had inspired his perfidy. His son, shocked and indignant, declined the proffered honors and emoluments that were only to be gained by an act of treason; and intimated his intention "to defend the Fort with his life, sooner than deliver it up to the enemies of his country." The father used the most earnest entreaties, the most touching and parental arguments. Charles Etienne was proof against these. The Baronet alluded to the large force under his command, and deplored the necessity of making an assault, in case his propositions were rejected. Charles Etienne only doubled his sentinels, and stood more firmly intrenched upon his honor. Then the elder La Tour ordered an assault. For two days the storm continued; sometimes the Mother-in-law led the Scotch soldiers to the breach, but the French soldiers, under the Daughter-in-law, drove them back with such bitter fury, that of the assailants it was hard to say which numbered most, the living or the dead. At last, La Tour the elder abandoned the siege; and "ashamed to appear in England, afraid to appear in France," accepted the humiliating alternative of requesting an asylum from his son. Permission to reside in the neighborhood was granted by Charles Etienne. The Scotch troops were reëmbarked for England; and the younger and the elder Mrs. de la Tour smiled at each other grimly from the plain and from the parapet. Further than this there was no intercourse between the families. Whenever Marie de la Tour sent the baby to grandmother, it went with a troop of cavalry and a flag of truce; and whenever Lady de la Tour left her card at the gate, the drums beat, and the guard turned out with fixed bayonets.

Such discipline had prepared Marie de la Tour for the heroic part which afterwards raised her to the historical position she occupies in the chronicles of Acadia. I have had occasion to speak of freedom of opinion existing in this Province—but for the invasion of English and Scotch filibusters, this absolute liberty of faith would have produced the happiest fruits in the new colonies. But unfortunately in a weak and newly-settled country, union in all things is an indispensable condition of existence. This very liberty of opinion, in a great measure disintegrated the early French settlements, and separated a people which otherwise might have encountered successfully its rapacious enemies.

At this time the French Governor of Acadia, Razillia, died. Charles Etienne la Tour as a subordinate officer, had full command of the eastern part of the province, as the Chevalier d'Aulney de Charnisé, had of the western portion, extending as far as the Penobscot. As for the Sterling patent, Sir William, finding it of little value, had sold it to the elder La Tour, but the defeated adventurer of Cape Sable by the treaty of St. Germains in 1632, was stripped of his new possessions by King Charles I., who conveyed the whole of the territory again to Louis XIII. of France. Thus it will be seen, that two claimants only were in possession of Acadia; namely, the younger La Tour and D'Aulney. The elder La Tour now retires from the scene, goes to England with his wife, and is heard of no more.

Between the rival commanders in Acadia, there were certain points of resemblance—both were youthful, both were brave, enterprising and ambitious, both the happy husbands of proud and beautiful wives. Otherwise La Tour was a Huguenot and D'Aulney a Catholic—thus it will be seen that the latter had the most favor at the French court, while the former could more securely count upon the friendship of the English of Massachusetts Bay—no inconsiderable allies as affairs then stood. Under such circumstances, it is not to be wondered at that there was a constant feud between the two young officers, and their young wives. The chronicles of the Pilgrims, the records of Bradford, Winthrop, Mather, and Hutchinson, are full of the exploits of these pugnacious heroes. At one time La Tour appears in person at Boston, to beat up recruits, as more than two hundred years after, another power attempted to raise a foreign legion, and, although the pilgrim fathers do not officially sanction the proceeding, yet they connive at it, and quote Scripture to warrant them. Close upon this follows a protest of D'Aulney, and with it the exhibition of a warrant from the French king for the arrest of La Tour. Upon this there is a meeting of the council and a treaty, offensive and defensive, made with D'Aulney.

Meanwhile, Marie de la Tour arrived at Boston from England, where she had been on a visit to her mother-in-law. The captain of the vessel upon which she had reëmbarked for the new world, having carried her to this city instead of to the river St. John, according to the letter of the charter, was promptly served with a summons by that lady to appear before the magistrates to show cause why he did it; and the consequence was, madame recovered damages to the amount of two thousand pounds in the Marine Court of the Modern Athens. With this sum in her pocket, she chartered a vessel for the river St. John, and arrived at a small fort belonging to her husband, on its banks, just in time to defend it against D'Aulney, who had rallied his forces for an attack upon it, during the absence of Charles Etienne.

Marie de la Tour at this time was one of the most beautiful women in the new world. She was not less than twenty, nor more than thirty years of age; her features had a charm beyond the limits of the regular; her eyes were expressive; her mouth intellectual; her complexion brown and clear, could pale or flush with emotions either tender or indignant. Before such a commandress D'Aulney de Charnisé set down his forces in the year 1644.

The garrison was small—the brave Charles Etienne absent in a distant part of the province. But the unconquerable spirit of the woman prevailed over these disadvantages. At the first attack by D'Aulney, the guns of the fort were directed with such consummate skill that every shot told. The besieger, with twenty killed and thirteen wounded, was only too happy to warp his frigate out of the leach of this lovely lady's artillery, and retire to Penobscot to refit for further operations. Again D'Aulney sailed up the St. John, with the intention of taking the place by assault. By land as by water, his forces were repulsed with great slaughter. A host of Catholic soldiers fell before a handful of Protestant guns, which was not surprising, as the cannon were well pointed, and loaded with grape and canister. For three days the French officer carried on the attack, and then again retreated. On the fourth day a Swiss hireling deserted to the enemy and betrayed the weakness of the garrison. D'Aulney, now confident of success, determined to take the fort by storm; but as he mounted the wall, the lovely La Tour, at the head of her little garrison, met the besiegers with such determined bravery, that again they were repulsed. That evening D'Aulney hung the traitorous Swiss, and proposed honorable terms, if the brave commandress would surrender. To these terms Marie assented, in the vain hope of saving the lives of the brave men who had survived; the remnants of her little garrison. But the perfidious D'Aulney, who, from the vigorous defence of the fort, had supposed the number of soldiers to have been greater, instead of feeling that admiration which brave men always experience when acts of valor are presented by an enemy, lost himself in an abyss of chagrin, to find he had been thrice defeated by a garrison so contemptible in numbers, and led by a *female*. To his eternal infamy let it be recorded, that pretending to have been deceived by the terms of capitulation, D'Aulney hanged the brave survivors of the garrison, and even had the baseness and cruelty to parade Madame de la Tour herself on the same scaffold, with the ignominious cord around her neck, as a reprieved criminal.

To quote the words of the chronicler: "The violent and unusual exertions which Madame la Tour had made, the dreadful fate of her household and followers, and the total wreck of his fortune, had such an effect that she died soon after this event."

So perished the beautiful, the brave, the faithful, the unfortunate! Shall I add that her besieger, D'Aulney, died soon after, leaving a bereaved but blooming widow? That Charles Etienne la Tour, to prevent further difficulties in the province, laid siege to that sad and sympathizing lady, not with flag and drum, shot and shell, but with the more effectual artillery of love? That Madame D'Aulney finally surrendered, and that Charles Etienne was wont to say to her, after the wedding: "Beloved, *your* husband and *my* wife have had their pitched battle, but let *us* live in peace for the rest of our days, my dear."

Quaint, old, mouldy Halifax seems more attractive after re-writing this portion of its early history. The defence of that little fort, with its slender garrison, by Madame la Tour, against the perfidious Charnisé, brings to mind other instances of female heroism, peculiar to the French people. It recalls the achievements of Joan of Arc, and Charlotte Corday. Not less, than these, in the scale of intrepid valor, are those of Marie de la Tour.

CHAPTER XV.

Bedford Basin—Legend of the two French Admirals—An Invitation to the Queen—Visit to the Prince's Lodge—A Touch of Old England—The Ruins.

The harbor of Chebucto, after stretching inland far enough to make a commodious and beautiful site for the great city of Halifax, true to the fine artistic taste peculiar to all bodies of water in the province, penetrates still further in the landscape, and broadens out into a superb land-locked lake, called Bedford Basin. The entrance to this basin is very narrow, and it has no other outlet. Oral tradition maintains that about a century ago a certain French fleet, lying in the harbor, surprised by the approach of a superior body of English men-of-war in the offing, weighed anchor and sailed up through this narrow estuary into the basin itself, deceived by seeing so much water there, and believing it to be but a twin harbor through which they could escape again to the open sea. And further, that the French Admiral finding himself caught in this net with no chance of escape, drew his sword, and placing the hilt upon the deck of his vessel, fell upon the point of the weapon, and so died.

This tradition is based partly upon fact; its epoch is one of the most interesting in the history of this province, and probably the turning point in the affairs of the whole northern continent. The suicide was an officer high in rank, the Duke d'Anville, who in 1746, after the first capture of Louisburgh, sailed from Brest with the most formidable fleet that had ever crossed the Atlantic, to re-take this famous fortress; then to re-take Annapolis, next to destroy Boston, and finally to *visit* the West Indies. But his squadron being dispersed by tempestuous weather, he arrived in Chebucto harbor with but a few ships, and not finding any of the rest of his fleet there, was so affected by this and other disasters on the voyage, that he destroyed himself. So says the *London Chronicle* of August 24th, 1758, from which I take this account. The French say he died of apoplexy, the English by poison. At all events, he was buried in a little island in the harbor, after a defeat by the elements of as great an armament as that of the Spanish Armada. Some idea of the disasters of this voyage may be formed from one fact, that from the time of the sailing of the expedition from Brest until its arrival at Chebucto, no less than 1,270 men died on the way from the plague. Many of the ships arriving after this sad occurrence, Vice-Admiral Destournelle endeavored to fulfill the object of the mission, and even with his crippled forces essay to restore the glory of France in the western hemisphere. But he being overruled by a council of war, plucked out his sword, and followed his commander, the Duke d'Anville. What might have come of it, had either admiral again planted the *fleur de lis* upon the bastions of Louisburgh?

But to return to the to-day of to-day. Bedford Basin is now rapidly growing in importance. The great Nova Scotia railway skirts the margin of its storied waters, and already suburban villas for Haligonian Sparrowgrasses, are being erected upon its banks.

I was much amused one morning, upon opening one of the Halifax papers, to find in its columns a most warm and hearty invitation from the editor to her majesty, Queen Victoria, soliciting her to visit the province, which, according to the editorial phraseology, would be, no doubt, as interesting as it was endeared to her, as the former residence of her gracious father, the Duke of Kent.

In the year 1798, just twenty years before her present majesty was born, the young Prince Edward was appointed Commander-in-Chief of the forces in British North America. Loyalty, then as now, was rampant in Nova Scotia, and upon the arrival of his Royal Highness, among other marks of compliment, an adjacent island, that at present rejoices in a governor and parliament of its own, was re-christened with the name it now bears, namely—Prince Edward's Island. But I am afraid Prince Edward was a sad reprobate in those days—at least, such is the record of tradition.

The article in the newspaper reminded me that somewhere upon Bedford Basin were the remains of the "Prince's Lodge;" so one afternoon, accompanied by a dear old friend, I paid this royal bower by Bendemeer's stream, a visit. Rattling through the unpaved streets of Halifax in a one horse vehicle, called, for obvious reasons, a "jumper," we were soon on the high-road towards the basin. Water of the intensest blue—hill-slopes, now cultivated, and anon patched with evergreens that look as black as squares upon a chess board, between the open, broken grounds—a fine road—a summer sky—an atmosphere spicy with whiffs of resinous odors, and no fog,—these are the features of our ride. Yonder is a red building, reflected in the water like the prison of Chillon, where some of our citizens were imprisoned during the war of 1812—ship captives doubtless! And here is the customary little English inn, where we stop our steed to let him cool, while the stout landlord, girt with a clean white apron, brings out to his thirsty travellers a brace of foaming, creamy glasses of "right h'English h'ale." Then remounting the jumper, we skirt the edge of the basin again, until a stately dome rises up before us on the road, which, as we approach, we see is supported by columns, and based upon a gentle promontory overhanging the water. This is the "Music House," where the Prince's band were wont to play in days "lang syne." Here we stop, and leaving our jumper in charge of a farmer, stroll over the grounds.

That peculiar arrangement of lofty trees, sweeping lawns, and graceful management of water, which forms the prevailing feature of English landscape gardening, was at once apparent. Although there were no trim walks, green hedges, or beds of flowers; although the whole place was ruined and neglected, yet the magic touch of art was not less visible to the practised eye. The art that concealed art, seemed to lend a charm to the sweet seclusion, without intruding upon or disturbing the intentions of nature.

Proceeding up the gentle slope that led from the gate, a number of columbines and rose-bushes scattered in wild profusion, indicated where once had been the Prince's garden. These, although now in bloom and teeming with flowers, have a vagrant, neglected air, like beauties that had ran astray, never to be reclaimed. A little further we come upon the ruins of a spacious mansion, and beyond these the remains of the library, with its tumbled-down bricks and timbers, choking up the stream that wound through the vice-regal domains: and here the bowling-green, yet fresh with verdure; here the fishing pavilion, leaning over an artificial lake, with an artificial island in the midst; and here are willows, and deciduous trees, planted by the Prince; and other rose-bushes and columbines scattered in wild profusion. I could not but admire the elegance and grace, which, even now, were so apparent, amid the ruins of the lodge, nor could I help recalling those earlier days, when the red-coats clustered around the gates, and the grounds were sparkling with lamps at night; when the band from the music-house woke the echoes with the clash of martial instruments, and the young Prince, with his gay gallants, and his powdered, patched, and painted Jezebels, held his brilliant court, with banner, music, and flotilla; with the array of soldiery, and the pageantry of ships-of-war, on Bedford Basin.

I stood by the ruins of a little stone bridge, which had once spanned the sparkling brook, and led to the Prince's library; I saw, far and near, the flaunting flowers of the now abandoned garden, and the distant columns of the silent music house, and I felt sad amid the desolation, although I knew not why. For wherefore should any one feel sad to see the temples of dissipation laid in the dust? For my own part, I am a poor casuist, but nevertheless, I do not think my conscience will suffer from this feeling. There is a touch of humanity in it, and always some germ of sympathy will bourgeon and bloom around the once populous abodes of men, whether they were tenanted by the pure or by the impure.

CHAPTER XVI.

The Last Night—Farewell Hotel Waverley—Friends Old and New—What followed the Marriage of La Tour le Borgne—Invasion of Col. Church.

Faint nebulous spots in the air, little red disks in a halo of fog, acquaint us that there are gas-lights this night in the streets of Halifax. Something new, I take it, this illumination? Carbonated hydrogen is a novelty as yet in Chebucto. But in this soft and pleasant atmosphere, I cannot but feel some regret at leaving my old quarters in the Hotel Waverley. If I feel how much there is to welcome me elsewhere, yet I do not forsake this queer old city—these strange, dingy, weather-beaten streets, without reluctance; and chiefly I feel that now I must separate from some old friends, and from some new ones too, whom I can ill spare. And if any of these should ever read this little book, I trust they will not think the less of me because of it. If the salient features of the province have sometimes appeared to me, a stranger, a trifle distorted, it may be that my own stand-point is defective. And so farewell! To-morrow I shall draw nearer homeward, by Windsor and the shores of the Gasperau, by Grand-Pré and the Basin of Minas. Candles, Henry! and books!

The marriage of La Tour to the widow of his deceased rival, for a time enabled that brave young adventurer to remain in quiet possession of the territory. But to the Catholic Court of France, a suspected although not an avowed Protestant, in commission, was an object of distrust. No matter what might have been his former services, indeed, his defence of Cape Sable had saved the French

206

possessions from the encroachments of the Sterling patent, yet he was heretic to the true faith, and therefore defenceless in an important point against the attacks of an enemy. Such a one was La Tour le Borgne, who professed to be a creditor of D'Aulney, and pressing his suit with all the ardor of bigotry and rapacity, easily succeeded in "obtaining a decree by which he was authorized to enter upon the possessions of his *deceased debtor*!" But the adherents of Charles Etienne did not readily yield to the new adventurer. They had tasted the sweets of religious liberty, and were not disposed to come within the arbitrary yoke without a struggle. Disregarding the "decree," they stood out manfully against the forces of Le Borgne. Again were Catholic French and Protestant French cannon pointed against each other in unhappy Acadia. But fort after fort fell beneath the new claimant's superior artillery, until La Tour le Borgne himself was met by a counter-force of bigotry, before which his own was as chaff to the fanning-mill. The man of England, Oliver Cromwell, had his little claim, too, in Acadia. Against his forces both the French commanders made but ineffectual resistance. Acadia for the third time fell into the hands of the English.

Now in the history of the world there is nothing more patent than this: that persecution in the name of religion, is only a ring of calamities, which ends sooner or later where it began. And this portion of its history can be cited as an example. Charles Etienne de la Tour, alienated by the unjust treatment of his countrymen, decided to accept the protection of his national enemy. As the heir of Sir Claude de la Tour, he laid claim to the Sterling grants (which it will be remembered had been ceded to his father by Sir

William Alexander after the unsuccessful attack upon Cape Sable,) and in conjunction with two English Puritans obtained a new patent for Acadia from the Protector, under the great seal, with the title of Sir Charles La Tour. Then Sir Thomas Temple (one of the partners in the Cromwell patent) purchased the interest of Charles Etienne in Acadia. Then came the restoration, and again Acadia was restored to France by Charles II. in 1668. But Sir Thomas having embarked all his fortune in the enterprise, was not disposed to submit to the arbitrary disposal of his property by this treaty; and therefore endeavored to evade its articles by making a distinction between such parts of the province as were supposed to constitute Acadia proper, and the other portions of the territory comprehended under the title of Nova Scotia. "This distinction being deemed frivolous," Sir Thomas was ordered to obey the letter of the treaty, and accordingly the *whole of Nova Scotia* was delivered up to the Chevalier de Grande Fontaine. During twenty years succeeding this event, Acadia enjoyed comparative repose, subject only to occasional visits of filibusters. At the expiration of that time, a more serious invasion was meditated. Under the command of Sir William Phipps, a native of New England, three ships, with transports and soldiers, appeared before Port Royal, and demanded an unconditional surrender. Although the fort was poorly garrisoned, this was refused by Manivel, the French governor, but finally terms of capitulation were agreed upon: these were, that the French troops should be allowed to retain their arms and baggage, and be carried to Quebec; that the inhabitants should be maintained in the peaceable possession of their property, and in the exercise of their religion; and that the honor of the women should be observed. Sir

William agreed to the conditions, but declined signing the articles, pompously intimating that the "word of a general was a better security than any document whatever." The French governor, deceived by this specious parade of language, took the New England filibuster at his word, and formally surrendered the keys of the fortress, according to the verbal contract. Again was poor Acadia the victim of her perfidious enemy. Sir William, disregarding the terms of the capitulation, and the "word of a general," violated the articles he had pledged his honor to maintain, disarmed and imprisoned the soldiers, sacked the churches, and gave the place up to all the ruthless cruelties and violences of a general pillage. Not only this, the too credulous Governor, Manivel, was himself imprisoned, plundered of money and clothes, and carried off on board the conqueror's frigate, with many of his unfortunate companions, to view the further spoliations of his countrymen. Many a peaceful Acadian village expired in flames during that coasting expedition, and to add to the miseries of the defenceless Acadians, two *piratical* vessels followed in the wake of the pious Sir William, and set fire to the houses, slaughtered the cattle, hanged the inhabitants, and deliberately burned up one whole family, whom they had shut in a dwelling-house for that purpose.

Soon after this, Sir William was rewarded with the governorship of New England, as Argall had been with that of Virginia, nearly a century before.

Now let it be remembered that in these expeditions, very little, if any, attempt was made by the invaders to colonize or reside on the lands they were so ready to lay waste and destroy. The mind of the species "Puritan," by rigid discipline hardened against all frivolous amusements, and insensible to the charms of the drama, and the splendors of the mimic spectacle, with its hollow shows of buckram, tinsel, and pasteboard, seems to have been peculiarly fitted to enjoy these more substantial enterprises, which, owing to the defenceless condition of the French province, must have appeared to the rigid Dudleys and Endicotts merely as a series of light and elegant pastimes.

Scarcely had Sir William Phipps returned to Boston, when the Chevalier Villabon came from France with troops and implements of war. On his arrival, he found the British flag flying at Port Royal, unsupported by an English garrison. It was immediately lowered from the flag-staff, the white flag of Louis substituted, and once more Acadia was under the dominion of her parental government.

Villabon, in a series of petty skirmishes, soon recovered the rest of the territory, which was only occupied at a few points by feeble New England garrisons, and, in conjunction with a force of Abenaqui Indians, laid siege to the fort at Pemaquid, on the Penobscot, and captured it. In this affair, as we have seen, the famous Baron Castine was engaged.

The capture of the fort at Pemaquid, led to a train of reprisals, conspicuous in which was an actor in the theatre of events who heretofore had not appeared upon the Acadian stage. This was Col. Church, a celebrated bushwhacker and Indian-fighter, of memorable account in the King Philip war.

In order to estimate truly the condition of the respective parties, we must remember the severe iron and gunpowder nature of the Puritan of New England, his prejudices, his dyspepsia; his high-peaked hat and ruff; his troublesome conscience and catarrh; his natural antipathies to Papists and Indians, from having been scalped by one, and roasted by both; his English insolence; and his religious bias, at once tyrannic and territorial.

Then, on the other, we must call to view the simple Acadian peasant, Papist or Protestant, just as it happened; ignorant of the great events of the world; a mere offshoot of rural Normandy; without a thought of other possessions than those he might reclaim from the sea by his dykes; credulous, pure-minded, patient of injuries; that like the swallow in the spring, thrice built the nest, and when again it was destroyed,

——"found the ruin wrought,But, not cast down, forth from the place it flew,And with its mate fresh earth and grasses brought,And built the nest anew."

Against such people, the expedition of Col. Church, fresh from the slaughter of Pequod wars, bent its merciless energies. Regardless of the facts that the people were non-resistants; that the expeditions of the French had been only feeble retaliations of great injuries; and always by levies from the mother country, and not from the colonists; that Villabon, at the capture of Pemaquid, had generously saved the lives of the soldiers in the garrison from the fury of the Mic-Macs, who had just grounds of retribution for the massacres which had marked the former inroads of these ruthless invaders; the wrath of the Pilgrim Fathers fell upon the unfortunate Acadians as though they had been a nation of Sepoys.[D]

One of the severest cruelties practised upon these inoffensive people, was that of requiring them to betray their friends, the Indians, under the heaviest penalties. In Acadia, the red and the white man were as brothers; no treachery, no broken faith, no over-reaching policy had severed the slightest fibre of good fellowship on either side. But the Abenaqui race was a warlike people. At the first invasion, under Argall, the red man had seen with surprise a mere handful of white men disputing for a territory to which neither could offer a claim; so vast as to make either occupation or control by the adventurers ridiculous; and therefore, with good-natured zeal, he had hastened to put an end to the quarrel, as though the white people had only been fractious but not irreconcilable kinsmen. But as the power of New England advanced more and more in Acadia, the first generous desire of the red man had merged into suspicion, and finally hatred of the peaked hat and ruff of Plymouth. In all his dealings with the Acadians, the Indian had found only unimpeachable faith and honor; but with the colonist of Massachusetts, there had been nothing but over-reaching and treachery: intercourse with the first had not led to a scratch, or a single drop of blood; while on the other hand a bounty of "one hundred pounds was offered for each male of their tribe if over twelve years of age, if scalped; one hundred and five pounds if taken prisoner; fifty pounds for each *woman and child scalped*, and fifty pounds when brought in alive."

The Abenaqui tribes therefore, first, to avenge the injuries of their unresisting friends, the Acadians, and after to avenge their own, waged war upon the invaders with all the severities of an aggrieved and barbarous people. And, as I have said before, the severest cruelty inflicted upon the Acadian colonist, was to oblige him to betray his best friend and protector, the painted heathen, with whom he struck hands and plighted faith. To the honor of these colonists, be it said, that although they saw their long years' labor of dykes broken down, the sea sweeping over their farms, the fire rolling about their homesteads, their cattle and sheep destroyed, their effects plundered, and wanton and nameless outrages committed by the English and Yankee soldiery, yet in no instance did they purchase indemnity from these, by betraying a single Indian.

CHAPTER XVII.

A few more Threads of History—Acadia again lost—The Oath of Allegiance—Settlement of Halifax—The brave Three Hundred—Massacre at Norridgewoack—Le Père Ralle.

During the invasion of Col. Church, the inhabitants of Grand-Pré were exposed to such treatment as may be conceived of. The smoke from the borders of the five rivers, overlooked by Blomidon, rose in the stilly air, and again the sea rolled past the broken dykes, which for nearly a century had kept out its desolating waters between the Cape and the Gasperau. Driven to despair, a few of the younger Acadians took up arms to defend their hearthstones, but the great body of the people submitted without resistance. A brief stand was made at Port Royal, but this last outpost finally capitulated. By the terms of the articles agreed upon, the inhabitants were to have the privilege of remaining upon their estates for two years, upon taking an oath of allegiance to remain faithful to her majesty, Queen Anne, during that period. Upon that consideration, those who lived *within cannon-shot* of the fort, were to be protected in their rights and properties. This was but a piece of *finesse* on the part of the invaders, an entering wedge, as it were, of a novel kind of tyranny, namely, that inasmuch as those within cannon-shot had taken the oath of allegiance, those without the reach of artillery, at Port Royal, also, were bound to do the same. And a strong detachment of New England troops, under Captain Pigeon, was sent upon an expedition to enforce the arbitrary oath. But Captain Pigeon, in the pursuit of his duty, fell in with an enemy of a less gentle nature than the Acadians. A body of Abenaqui came down upon him and his men, and smote them hip and thigh, even as the three hundred warriors of Israel smote the Midianites in the valley of Moreh. Then was there temporary relief in the land until the year 1713, when by a treaty Acadia was formally surrendered to England. The weight of the oath of allegiance now fell heavily upon the innocent colonists. We can scarcely appreciate the abhorrence of a people, so conscientious as this, to take an oath of fidelity to a race that had only been known to them by its rapacity. But partly by persuasion, partly by menace, a majority of the Acadians took the oath, which was as follows:

"Je promets et jure sincèrement, en foi de Chrétien, que je serai entièrement fidèle et obéirai vraiment sa Majesté le roi George, que je reconnaîs pour le Souverain seigneur de l'Acadie, ou Nouvelle Ecosse, ainsi Dieu me soit en aide."

Under the shadow of the protection derived from their acceptance of this oath, the Acadians reposed a few years. It did not oblige them to bear arms against their countrymen, nor did it compromise their religious independence of faith. Again the dykes were built to resist the encroachments of the sea; again village after village arose—at the mouth of the Gasperau, on the shores of the Canard, beside the Strait of Frontenac, at Le Have, and Rossignol, at Port Royal and Pisiquid. During all these years no attempt had been made by the captors of this province, to colonize the places baptized with the waters of Puritan progress. Lunenburgh was settled with King William's Dutchmen; the walls of Louisburgh were rising in one of the harbors of a neighboring island; but in no instance had the filibusters projected a *colony* on the soil which had been wrested from its rightful owners. The only result of all their bloody visitations upon a non-resisting people, had been to make defenceless Acadia a neutral province. From this time until the close of the drama, in all the wars between the Georges and the Louises, in both hemispheres, the people of Acadia went by the name of "The Neutral French."

Meantime the walls of Louisburgh were rising on the island of Cape Breton, which, with Canada, still remained under the sovereign rule of the French. The Acadians were invited to remove within the protection of this formidable fortress, but they preferred remaining intrenched behind their dykes, firmly believing that the only invader they had now to dread was the sea, inasmuch as they had accepted the oath of fidelity, in which, and in their inoffensive pursuits, they imagined themselves secure from farther molestation. Some of their Indian neighbors, however, accepted the invitation of the Cape Breton French, and removed thither. These simple savages, notwithstanding the changes in the government, still regarded the Acadians as friends, and the English as enemies. They could not comprehend the nature of a treaty by which their own lands were ceded to a hostile force; a treaty in which they were neither consulted nor considered.[E] They had their own injuries to remember, which in no wise had been balanced in the compact of the strangers. The rulers in New France (so says the chronicler) "affected to consider the Indians as an independent people." At Canseau, at Cape Sable, at Annapolis, and Passamaquoddy, English forts, fishing stations, and vessels were attacked and destroyed by the savages with all the circumstances that make up the hideous features of barbaric reprisal. Unhappy Acadia came in for her share of condemnation.

Although her innocent people had no part in these transactions, yet her missionaries had converted the Abenaqui to faith in the symbol of the crucifixion, and it was currently reported and credited in New England, that they had taught the savages to believe also the English were the people who had crucified our Saviour. To complicate matters again, the Chevalier de St. George (of whom there is no recollection except that he was anonymous, both as a prince, and as a man) sent his son, the fifth remove in stupidity, of the most stupid line of monarchs (not even excepting the Georges) that ever wore crowns, to stir up an insurrection among the most obtuse race of people that ever wore, or went without, breeches. A war between France and England followed the descent of the Pretender. A war naturally followed in the Colonies.

Again the ring of fire and slaughter met and ended in a treaty; the treaty of Aix la Chapelle, by which Cape Breton was ceded to France, and Nova Scotia, or Acadia, to England. Up to this time no attempt at colonizing the fertile valleys of Acadia, by its captors, had been attempted. At last, under large and favorable grants from the Crown, a colony was established by the Hon. Edward Cornwallis, at a place now known as Halifax. No sooner was Halifax settled, than sundry tribes of red men made predatory visits to the borders of the new colony. Reprisals followed reprisals, and it is not easy to say on which side lay the largest amount of savage fury. At the same time, the Acadians remained true to the spirit and letter of the oath they had taken. "They had relapsed," says the chronicler, "into a sort of sullen neutrality." This was considered just cause of offence. The oath which had satisfied Governor Phipps, did not satisfy George II. A new oath of allegiance was tendered, by which the Acadians were required to become loyal subjects of the English Crown, to bear arms against their countrymen, and the Indians to whom the poor colonists were bound by so many ties of obligation and affection. The consciences of these simple people revolted at a requisition "so repugnant to the feelings of human nature." Three hundred of the younger and braver Acadians took up arms against their oppressors. This overt act was just what was desired by the wily Puritans. Acadia, with its twenty thousand inhabitants, was placed under the ban of having violated the oath of neutrality in the persons of the three hundred. In vain the great body of the people protested that this act was contrary to their wishes, their peaceful habits, and beyond their control. At the fort of Beau Séjour, the brave three hundred made a gallant stand, but were defeated. Would there had been a Leonidas among them! Would that the whole of their kinsmen had erected forts instead of dykes, and dropped the plough-handles to press the edge of the sabre against the grindstone! Sad indeed is the fate of that people who make any terms with such an enemy, except such as may be granted at the bayonet's point. Sad indeed is the condition of that people who are wrapt in security when Persecution steals in upon them, hiding its bloody hands under the garments of sanctity.

Among the many incidents of these cruel wars, the fate of a Jesuit priest may stand as a type of the rest. Le Père Ralle had been a missionary for forty years among the various tribes of the Abenaqui. "His literary attainments were of a high order;" his knowledge of modern languages respectable; "his Latin," according to Haliburton, "was pure, classical and elegant;" and he was master of several of the Abenaqui dialects; indeed, a manuscript dictionary of the Abenaqui languages, in his handwriting, is still preserved in the library of the Harvard University. Of one of these tribes—the Norridgewoacks—Father Ralle was the pastor. Its little village was on the banks of the Kennebeck; the roof of its tiny chapel rose above the pointed wigwams of the savages; and a huge cross, the emblem of peace, lifted itself above all, the conspicuous feature of the settlement in the distance. By the tribe over which he had exercised his gentle rule for so many years, Le Père Ralle was regarded with superstitious reverence and affection.

It does not appear that these people had been accused of any overt acts; but, nevertheless, the village was marked out for destruction. Two hundred and eight Massachusetts men were dispatched upon this errand. The settlement was surprised at night, and a terrible scene of slaughter ensued. Ralle came forth from his chapel to save, if possible, the lives of his miserable parishioners. "As soon as he was seen," says the chronicler,[F] "he was saluted with a great shout and a shower of bullets, and fell, together with seven Indians, who had rushed out of their tents to defend him with their bodies; and when the pursuit ceased, the Indians who had fled, returned to weep over their beloved missionary, and found him dead at the foot of the cross, his body perforated with balls, his head scalped, his skull broken with blows of hatchets, his mouth and eyes filled with mud, the bones of his legs broken, and his limbs dreadfully mangled. After having bathed his remains with their tears, they buried him on the site of the chapel, that had been hewn down with its crucifix, with whatever else remained of the emblems of idolatry." Such was the merciless character of the invasion of Acadia; such the looming phantom of the greater crime which was so speedily to spread ruin over her fair valleys, and scatter forever her pastoral people.

The tranquillity of entire subjugation followed these events in the province. The New Englander built his menacing forts along the rivers, and pressed into his service the labors of the neutral French. "The requisitions which were made of them were not calculated to conciliate affection," says the chronicler; the poor Acadian peasant was informed, if he did not supply the garrison fuel, his own house would be used for that purpose, and that neglect to furnish timber for the repairs of a fort, would be followed by drum-head courts martial, and "military execution."

To all these exactions, these unhappy people patiently submitted. But in vain. The very existence of the subjugated race had become irksome to their oppressors. A cruelty yet more intolerable to which the history of the world affords no parallel, remained to be perpetrated.

CHAPTER XVIII.

On the road to Windsor—The great Nova Scotia Railway—A Fellow Passenger—Cape Sable Shipwrecks—Seals—Ponies—Windsor—Sam Slick—A lively Example.

A dewy, spring-like morning is all I remembered of my farewell to Halifax. A very sweet and odorous air as I rode towards the railway station in the funereal cab; a morning without fog, a sparkling freshness that twinkled in the leaves and crisped the waters.

So I take leave of thee, quaint old city of Chebucto. The words of a familiar ditty, the memory of the unfortunate Miss Bailey, rises upon me as the morning bugle sounds—

"A captain bold in Halifax, who lived in country quarters,Seduced a maid, who hung herself next morning in her garters;His wicked conscience smoted him, he lost his spirits daily,He took to drinking ratifia, and thought upon Miss Bailey."

While the psychological features of the case were puzzling his brain and keeping him wide awake—

"The candles blue, at XII. o'clock, began to burn quite paley,A ghost appeared at his bedside, and said—behold, Miss Bailey!!!"

Even such a sprite, so dead in look, so woe-begone, drew Priam's curtain in the dead of night to tell him half his Troy was burned; but this visit was for a different purpose, as we find by the words which the gallant Lothario addressed to his victim:

"'You'll find,' says he, 'a five-pound note in my regimental small-clothes;'T will bribe the sexton for your grave,' the ghost then vanished gaily.Saying, 'God bless you, wicked Captain Smith, although you've ruined Miss Bailey.'"

There is no end to these legends; the whole province is full of them. The Province Building is stuffed with rich historical manuscripts, that only wait for the antiquarian explorer.[G]

But now we approach the station of the great Nova Scotia Railway, nine and three-quarter miles in length, that skirts the margin of Bedford Basin, and ends at the head of that blue sheet of water in the village of Sackville. It is amusing to see the gravity and importance of the conductor, in uniform frock-coat and with crown and V. R. buttons, as he paces up and down the platform before starting; and the quiet dignity of the sixpenny ticket-office; and the busy air of the freight-master, checking off boxes and bundles for the distant terminus—so distant that it can barely be distinguished by the naked eye. But it was a pleasant ride, that by the Basin! Not less pleasant because of the company of an old friend, who, with wife and children, went with me to the end of the iron road. Arrived there, we parted, with many a hearty hand-shake, and thence by stage to Windsor, on the river Avon, forty-five miles or so west of Halifax.

My fellow-passenger on the stage-top was a pony! Yes, a real pony! not bigger, however, than a good sized pointer dog, although his head was of most preposterous horse-like length. This equine Tom Thumb, was one of the mustangs, or wild horses of Sable Island, some little account of which here may not be uninteresting. But first let me say, in order not to tax the credulity of my reader too much, that pony did not stand upright upon the roof of the coach, as may have been surmised, but was very cleverly laid upon his side, with his four legs strapped in the form of a saw-buck, precisely as butchers tie the legs of calves or of sheep together, for transportation in carts to the shambles, only pony's fetters were not so cruel—indeed he seemed to be quite at his ease—like the member of the foreign legion on the road to Dartmouth.

Now then, pony's birth-place is one of the most interesting upon our coast. Do you remember it, my transatlantic traveller? The little yellow spot that greets you so far out at sea, and bids you welcome to the western hemisphere? I hope you have seen it in fine weather; many a goodly ship has left her bones upon that yellow island in less auspicious seasons. The first of these misadventurers was Sir Humphrey Gilbert, who was lost in a storm close by; the memorable words with which he hailed his consort are now familiar to every reader: "Heaven," said he, "is as near by sea as by land," and so bade the world farewell in the tempest. Legends of wrecks of buccaneers, of spectres, multiply as we penetrate into the mysterious history of the yellow island. And its present aspect is sufficiently tempting to the adventurous, for whom—

"If danger other charms have none,Then danger's self is lure alone."

The following description, from a lecture delivered in Halifax, by Dr. J. Bernard Gilpin, will commend itself to our modern Robinson Crusoes:

"Should any one be visiting the island now, he might see, about ten miles' distance, looking seaward, half a dozen low, dark hummocks on the horizon. As he approaches, they gradually resolve themselves into hills fringed by breakers, and by and by the white sea beach with its continued surf—the sand-hills, part naked, part waving in grass of the deepest green, unfold themselves—a house and a barn dot the western extremity—here and there along the wild beach lie the ribs of unlucky traders half-buried in the shifting sand. By this time a red ensign is waving at its peak, and from a tall flag-staff and crow's nest erected upon the highest hill midway of the island, an answering flag is waving to the wind. Before the anchor is let go, and the cutter is rounding to in five fathoms of water, men and horses begin to dot the beach, a life-boat is drawn rapidly on a boat-cart to the beach, manned, and fairly breasting the breakers upon the bar. It may have been three long winter months that this boat's crew have had no tidings of the world, or they may have three hundred emigrants and wrecked crews, waiting to be carried off. The hurried greetings over, news told and newspapers and letters given, the visitor prepares to return with them to the island. Should it be evening, he will see the cutter already under weigh and standing seaward; but, should it be fine weather, plenty of day, and wind right off the shore, even then she lies to the wind anchor apeak, and mainsail hoisted, ready to run at a moment's notice, so sudden are the shifts of wind, and so hard to claw off from those treacherous shores. But the life-boat is now entering the perpetual fringe of surf—a few seals tumble and play in the broken waters, and the stranger draws his breath hard, as the crew bend to their oars, the helmsman standing high in the pointed stern, with loud command and powerful arm keeping her true, the great boat goes riding on the back of a huge wave, and is carried high up on the beach in a mass of struggling water. To spring from their seats into the water, and hold hard the boat, now on the point of being swept back by the receding wave, is the work of an instant. Another moment they are left high and dry on the beach, another, and the returning wave and a vigorous run of the crew has borne her out of all harm's way.

"Such is the ceremony of landing at Sable Island nine or ten months out of the year: though there are at times some sweet halcyon days when a lad might land in a flat. Dry-shod the visitor picks his way between the thoroughly drenched crew, picks up a huge scallop or two, admires the tumbling play of the round-headed seals, and plods his way through the deep sand of an opening between the hills, or gulch (so called) to the head-quarters establishment. And here, for the last fifty years, a kind welcome has awaited all, be they voluntary idlers or sea-wrecked men. Screened by the sand-hills, here is a well-stocked barn and barnyard, filled with its ordinary inhabitants, sleek milch cows and heady bulls, lazy swine, a horse grazing at a tether, with geese and ducks and fowls around. Two or three large stores and boat-houses, quarters for the men, the Superintendent's house, blacksmith shop, sailors' home for sea-wrecked men, and oil-house, stand around an irregular square, and surmounted by the tall flag-staff and crow's nest on the neighboring hill. So abrupt the contrast, so snug the scene, if the roar of the ocean were out of his ears, one might fancy himself twenty miles inland.

"Nearly the first thing the visitor does is to mount the flag-staff, and climbing into the crow's nest, scan the scene. The ocean bounds him everywhere. Spread east and west, he views the narrow island in form of a bow, as if the great Atlantic waves had bent it around, nowhere much above a mile wide, twenty-six miles long, including the dry bars, and holding a shallow late thirteen miles long in its centre.

"There it all lies spread like a map at his feet—grassy hill and sandy valley fading away into the distance. On the foreground the outpost men galloping their rough ponies into head-quarters, recalled by the flag flying above his head; the West-end house of refuge, with bread and matches, firewood and kettle, and directions to find water, and head-quarters with flag-staff on the adjoining hill. Every sandy peak or grassy knoll with a dead man's name or old ship's tradition—Baker's Hill, Trott's Cove, Scotchman's Head, French Gardens—traditionary spot where the poor convicts expiated their social crimes—the little burial-ground nestling in the long grass of a high hill, and consecrated to the repose of many a sea-tossed limb; and two or three miles down the shallow lake, the South-side house and barn, and staff and boats lying on the lake beside the door. Nine miles further down, by the help of a glass, he may view the flag-staff at the foot of the lake, and five miles further the East-end look-out, with its staff and watch-house. Herds of wild ponies dot the hills, and black duck and sheldrakes are heading their young broods on the mirror-like ponds. Sealsinnumerable are basking on the warm sands, or piled like ledges of rock along the shores. The Glascow's bow, the Maskonemet's stern, the East Boston's hulk, and the grinning ribs of the well-fastened Guide are spotting the sands, each with its tale of last adventure, hardships passed, and toil endured. The whole picture is set in a silver-frosted frame of rolling surf and sea-ribbed sand."

The patrol duty of the hardy islander is thus described:

"Mounted upon his hardy pony, the solitary patrol starts upon his lonely way. He rides up the centre valleys, ever and anon mounting a grassy hill to look seaward, reaches the West-end bar, speculates upon perchance a broken spar, an empty bottle, or a cask of beef struggling in the land-wash—now fords the shallow lake, looking well for his land-range, to escape the hole where Baker was drowned; and coming on the breeding-ground of the countless birds, his pony's hoof with a reckless smash goes crunching through a dozen eggs or callow young. He fairly puts his pony to her mettle to escape the cloud of angry birds which, arising in countless numbers, dent his weather-beaten tarpaulin with their sharp bills, and snap his pony's ears, and confuse him with their sharp, shrill cries. Ten minutes more, and he is holding hard to count the seals. There they lie, old ocean flocks, resting their wave-tossed limbs—great ocean bulls, and cows, and calves. He marks them all. The wary old male turns his broad moustached nostrils to the tainted gale of man and horse sweeping down upon them, and the whole herd are simultaneously lumbering a retreat. And now he goes, plying his little short whip, charging the whole herd to cut off their retreat for the pleasure and fun of galloping in and over and amongst fifty great bodies, rolling and tumbling and tossing, and splashing the surf in their awkward endeavors to escape."

And now to return to our pony, who seems to sympathize with his fellow-traveller, for every instant he raises his head as if he would peep into his note-book. Let me quote this of him and of his brethren:

"When the present breed of wild ponies was introduced, there is no record. In an old print, seemingly a hundred years old, they are depicted as being lassoed by men in cocked hats and antique habiliments. At present, three or four hundred are their utmost numbers, and it is curious to observe how in their figures and habits they approach the wild races of Mexico or the Ukraine. They are divided into herds or gangs, each having a separate pasture, and each presided over by an old male, conspicuous by the length of his mane, rolling in tangled masses over eye and ear down to his fore arm. Half his time seems taken up in tossing it from his eyes as he collects his out-lying mares and foals on the approach of strangers, and keeping them well up in a pack boldly faces the enemy whilst they retreat at a gallop. If pressed, however, he, too, retreats on their rear. He brooks no undivided allegiance, and many a fierce battle is waged by the contending chieftains for the honor of the herd. In form they resemble the wild horses of all lands: the large head, thick, shaggy neck of the male, low withers, paddling gait, and sloping quarters, have all their counterparts in the mustang and the horse of the Ukraine. There seems a remarkable tendency in these horses to assume the Isabella colors, the light chestnuts, and even the piebalds or paint horses of the

Indian prairies or the Mexican Savannah. The annual drive or herding, usually resulting in the whole island being swept from end to end, and a kicking, snorting, half-terrified mass driven into a larg pound, from which two or three dozen are selected, lassoed, and exported to town, affords fine sport, wild riding, and plenty of falls."

Thus much for Sable Island.

"Dark isle of mourning! aptly art thou named,For thou hast been the cause of many a tear;For deeds of treacherous strife too justly famed,The Atlantic's charnel—desolate and drear;A thing none love, though wand'ring thousands fear—If for a moment rest the Muse's wingWhere through the waves thy sandy wastes appear,'Tis that she may one strain of horror sing,Wild as the dashing waves that tempests o'er thee fling."[H]

And now pony we must part. Windsor approaches! Yonder among the embowering trees is the residence of Judge Halliburton, the author of "Sam Slick." How I admire him for his hearty hostility to republican institutions! It is natural, straightforward, shrewd, and, no doubt, sincere. At the same time, it affords an example of how much the colonist or satellite form of government tends to limit the scope of the mind, which under happier skies and in a wider intelligence might have shone to advantage.

CHAPTER XIX.

Windsor-upon-Avon—Ride to the Gasperau—The Basin of Minas—Blomidon—This is the Acadian Land—Basil, the Blacksmith—A Yankee Settlement—Useless Reflections.

Windsor lies upon the river Avon. It is not the Avon which runs by Stratford's storied banks, but still it is the Avon. There is something in a name. Witness it, O river of the Blue Noses!

I cannot recall a prettier village than this. If you doubt my word, come and see it. Yonder we discern a portion of the Basin of Minas; around us are the rich meadows of Nova Scotia. Intellect has here placed a crowning college upon a hill; opulence has surrounded it with picturesque villas. A ride into the country, a visit to a bachelor's lodge, studded with horns of moose and cariboo, with woodland scenes and Landseer's pictures, and then— over the bridge, and over the Avon, towards Grand-Pré and the Gasperau! I suppose, by this time, my dear reader, you are tired of sketches of lake scenery, mountain scenery, pines and spruces, strawberry blossoms, and other natural features of the province? For my part, I rode through a strawberry-bed three hundred miles long—from Sydney to Halifax—diversified by just such patches of scenery, and was not tired of it. But it is a different matter when you come to put it on paper. So I forbear.

Up hill we go, soon to approach the tragic theatre. A crack of the whip, a stretch of the leaders, and now, suddenly, the whole valley comes in view! Before us are the great waters of Minas; yonder Blomidon bursts upon the sight; and below, curving like a scimitar around the edge of the Basin, and against the distant cliffs that shut out the stormy Bay of Fundy, is the Acadian land—the idyllic meadows of Grand-Pré lie at our feet.

The Abbé Reynal's account of the colony, as it appeared one hundred years ago, I take from the pages of Haliburton:

"Hunting and fishing, which had formerly been the delight of the colony, and might have still supplied it with subsistence, had no further attraction for a simple and quiet people, and gave way to agriculture, which had been established in the marshes and low lands, by repelling with dykes the sea and rivers which covered these plains. These grounds yielded fifty for one at first, and afterwards fifteen or twenty for one at least; wheat and oats succeeded best in them, but they likewise produced rye, barley and maize. There were also potatoes in great plenty, the use of which was become common. At the same time these immense meadows were covered with numerous flocks. They computed as many as sixty thousand head of horned cattle; and most families had several horses, though the tillage was carried on by oxen. Their habitations, which were constructed of wood, were extremely convenient, and furnished as neatly as substantial farmer's houses in Europe. They reared a great deal of poultry of all kinds, which made a variety in their food, at once wholesome and plentiful. Their ordinary drink was beer and cider, to which they sometimes added rum. Their usual clothing was in general the produce of their own flax, or the fleeces of their own sheep; with these they made common linens and coarse cloths. If any of them had a desire for articles of greater luxury, they procured them from Annapolis or Louisburg, and gave in exchange corn, cattle or furs. The neutral French had nothing else to give their neighbors, and made still fewer exchanges among themselves; because each separate family was able, and had been accustomed to provide for its own wants. They therefore knew nothing of paper currency, which was so common throughout the rest of North America. Even the small quantity of gold and silver which had been introduced into the colony, did not inspire that activity in which consists its real value. Their manners were of course extremely simple. There was seldom a cause, either civil or criminal, of importance enough to be carried before the Court of Judication, established at Annapolis. Whatever little differences arose from time to time among them, were amicably adjusted by their elders. All their public acts were drawn by their pastors, who had likewise the keeping of their wills; for which, and their religious services, the inhabitants paid a twenty-seventh part of their harvest, which was always sufficient to afford more means than there were objects of generosity.

"Real misery was wholly unknown, and benevolence anticipated the demands of poverty.[1] Every misfortune was relieved, as it were, before it could be felt, without ostentation on the one hand, and without meanness on the other. It was, in short, a society of brethren; every individual of which was equally ready to give, and to receive, what he thought the common right of mankind. So perfect a harmony naturally prevented all those connections of gallantry which are so often fatal to the peace of families. This evil was prevented by early marriages, for no one passed his youth in a state of celibacy. As soon as a young man arrived to the proper age, the community built him a house, broke up the lands about it, and supplied him with all the necessaries of life for a twelvemonth. There he received the partner whom he had chosen, and who brought him her portion in flocks. This new family grew and prospered like the others. In 1755, all together made a population of eighteen thousand souls. Such is the picture of these people, as drawn by the Abbé Reynal. By many, it is thought to represent a state of social happiness totally inconsistent with the frailties and passions of human nature, and that it is worthy rather of the poet than the historian. In describing a scene of rural felicity like this, it is not improbable that his narrative has partaken of the warmth of feeling for which he was remarkable; but it comes much nearer the truth than is generally imagined. Tradition is fresh and positive in the various parts of the United States where they were located respecting their guileless, peaceable, and scrupulous character; and the descendants of those, whose long cherished and endearing local attachment induced them to return to the land of their nativity, still deserve the name of a mild, frugal, and pious people."

As we rest here upon the summit of the Gasperau Mountain, and look down on yonder valley, we can readily imagine such a people. A pastoral people, rich in meadow-lands, secured by laborious dykes, and secluded from the struggling outside world. But we miss the thatch-roof cottages, by hundreds, which should be the prominent feature in the picture, the vast herds of cattle, the belfries of scattered village chapels, the murmur of evening fields,

"Where peace was tinkling in the shepherd's bell, And singing with the reapers."

233

These no longer exist:

"Naught but tradition remains of the beautiful village of Grand-Pré."

I sank back in the stage as it rolled down the mountain-road, and fairly covered my eyes with my hands, as I repeated Webster's boast: "Thank God! I too am an American." "But," said I, recovering, "thank God, I belong to a State that hasnever bragged much of its great moral antecedents!" and in that reflection I felt comforted, and the load on my back a little lightened.

A few weeping willows, the never-failing relics of an Acadian settlement, yet remain on the roadside; these, with the dykes and Great Prairie itself, are the only memorials of a once happy people. The sun was just sinking behind the Gasperau mountain as we entered the ancient village. There was a smithy beside the stage-house, and we could see the dusky glow of the forge within, and the swart mechanic

"Take in his leathern lap the hoof of the horse as a plaything, Nailing the shoe in its place."

But it was not Basil the Blacksmith, nor one of his descendants, that held the horse-hoof. The face of the smith was of the genuine New England type, and just such faces as I saw everywhere in the village. In the shifting panorama of the itinerary I suddenly found myself in a hundred-year-old colony of genuine Yankees, the real true blues of Connecticut, quilted in amidst the blue noses of Nova Scotia.

But of the poor Acadians not one remains now in the ancient village. It is a solemn comment upon their peaceful and unrevengeful natures, that two hundred settlers from New England remained unmolested upon their lands, and that the descendants of those New England settlers now occupy them. A solemn comment upon our history, and the touching epitaph of an exterminated race.

Much as we may admire the various bays and lakes, the inlets, promontories, and straits, the mountains and woodlands of this rarely-visited corner of creation—and, compared with it, we can boast of no coast scenery so beautiful—the valley of Grand-Pré transcends all the rest in the Province. Only our valley of Wyoming, as an inland picture, may match it, both in beauty and tradition. One has had its Gertrude, the other its Evangeline. But Campbell never saw Wyoming, nor has Longfellow yet visited the shores of the Basin of Minas. And I may venture to say, neither poet has touched the key-note of divine anger which either story might have awakened.

But let us be thankful for those simple and beautiful idyls. After all, it is a question whether the greatest and noblest impulses of man are not awakened rather by the sympathy we feel for the oppressed, than by the hatred engendered by the acts of the oppressor?

I wish I could shake off these useless reflections of a bygone period. But who can help it?

"This is the forest primeval; but where are the hearts that beneath it Leaped like the roe when it hears in the woodland the voice of the huntsman? Where is the thatch-roof village, the home of Acadian farmers—Men whose lives glided on like rivers that water the woodlands? Waste are those pleasant farms, and the farmers forever departed!"

CHAPTER XX.

The Valley of Acadia—A Morning Ride to the Dykes—An unexpected Wild-duck Chase—High Tides—The Gasperau—Sunset—The Lamp of History—Conclusion.

The eastern sun glittered on roof and window-pane next morning. Neat houses in the midst of trim gardens, rise tier above tier on the hill-slopes that overlook the prairie lands. A green expanse, several miles in width, extends to the edge of the dykes, and in the distance, upon its verge, here and there a farmhouse looms up in the warm haze of a summer morning. On the left hand the meadows roll away until they are merged in the bases of the cliffs that, stretching forth over the blue water of the Basin, end abruptly at Cape Blomidon. These cliffs are precise counterparts of our own Palisades, on the Hudson. Then to the right, again, the vision follows the hazy coast-line until it melts in the indistinct outline of wave and vapor, back of which rises the Gasperau mountain, that protects the valley on the east with corresponding barriers of rock and forest. Within this hemicycle lie the waters of Minas, bounded on the north by the horizon-line, the clouds and the sky.

Once happy Acadia nestled in this valley. Does it not seem incredible that even Puritan tyranny could have looked with hard and pitiless eyes upon such a scene, and invade with rapine, sword and fire, the peace and serenity of a land so fair?

A morning ride across the Grand-Pré convinced me that the natural opulence of the valley had not been exaggerated. These once desolate and bitter marshes, reclaimed from the sea by the patient labor of the French peasant, are about three miles broad by twenty miles long. The prairie grass, even at this time of year, is knee-deep, and, as I was informed, yields, without cultivation, from two to four tons to the acre. The fertility of the valley in other respects is equally great. The dyke lands are intersected by a network of white causeways, raised above the level of the meadows. We passed over these to the outer edge of the dykes. "These lands," said my young companion, "are filled in this season with immense flocks of all kinds of feathered game." And I soon had reason to be convinced of the truth of it, for just then we started up what seemed to be a wounded wild-duck, upon which out leaped my companion from the wagon and gave chase. A bunch of tall grass, upon the edge of a little pool, lay between him and the game; he brushed hastily through this, and out of it poured a little feathered colony. As these young ones were not yet able to fly, they were soon captured—seven little black ducks safely nestled together under the seat of the wagon, and poor Niobe trailed her broken wing within a tempting distance in vain.

We were soon upon the dykes themselves, which are raised upon the edge of the meadows, and are quite insignificant in height, albeit of great extent otherwise. But from the bottom of the dykes to the edge of yonder sparkling water, there is a bare beach, full three miles in extent. What does this mean? What are these dykes for, if the enemy is so far off? The answer to this query discloses a remarkable phenomenon. The tide in this part of the world rises sixty or seventy feet every twelve hours. At present the beach is bare; the five rivers of the valley—the Gasperau, the Cornwallis, the

Canard, the Habitant, the Perot—are empty. Betimes the tide will roll in in one broad unretreating wave, surging and shouldering its way over the expanse, filling all the rivers, and dashing against the protecting barriers under our feet; but before sunset the rivers will be emptied again, the bridges will uselessly hang in the air over the deserted channels, the beach will yawn wide and bare where a ship of the line might have anchored. Sometimes a stranger schooner from New England, secure in a safe distance from shore, drops down in six or seven fathom. Then, suddenly, the ebb sweeps off from the intruder, and leaves his two-master keeled over, with useless anchor and cable exposed, "to point a moral and adorn a tale." Sometimes a party will take boat for a row upon the placid bosom of this bay; but woe unto them if they consult not the almanac! A mistake may leave them high and dry on the beach, miles from the dykes, and as the tide comes in with a *bore*, a sudden influx, wave above wave, the risk is imminent.

I passed two days in this happy valley, sometimes riding across to the dykes, sometimes visiting the neighboring villages, sometimes wandering on foot over the hills to the upper waters of the rivers. And the Gasperau in particular is an attractive little mountain sylph, as it comes skipping down the rocks, breaking here and there out in a broad cascade, or rippling and singing in the heart of the grand old forest. I think my friend Kensett might set his pallet here, and pitch a brief tent by Minas and the Gasperau to advantage. For my own part, I would that I had my trout-pole and a fly!

But now the sun sinks behind the cliffs of Blow-me-down. To-morrow I must take the steamer for home, "sweet home!" What shall I say in conclusion? Shall I stop here and write *finis*, or once more trim the lamp of history? I feel as it were the whole wrongs of the French Province concentrated here, as in the last drop of its life blood, no tender dream of pastoral description, no clever veil of elaborate verse, can conceal the hideous features of this remorseless act, this wanton and useless deed of New England cruelty. Do not mistake me, my reader. Do not think that I am prejudiced against New England. But I hate tyranny—under whatever disguise, or in whatever shape—in an individual, or in a nation—in a state, or in a congregation of states; so do you; and of course you will agree with me, that so long as the maxim obtains, "that the object justifies the means," certain effects must follow, and this maxim was the guiding star of our forefathers when they marched into the French province.

The peculiar situation of the Acadians, embarrassed the colonists of Massachusetts. The French *neutrals*, had taken the oath of fidelity, but they refused to take the oath of allegiance which compelled them to bear arms against their countrymen, and the Indians, who from first to last had been their constant and devoted friends. The long course of persecution, for a century and a half, had struck but one spark of resistance from this people—the stand of the three hundred young warriors at Fort Séjour. Upon this act followed the retaliation of the Pilgrim Fathers. They determined to remove and disperse the Acadians among the British colonies. To carry out this edict, Colonel Winslow, with five transports and a sufficient force of New England troops, was dispatched to the Basin of Minas. At a consultation, held between Colonel Winslow and Captain Murray, it was agreed that a proclamation should be issued at the different settlements, requiring the attendance of the people at the respective posts on the same day; which proclamation would be so ambiguous in its nature, that the object for which they were to assemble could not be discerned, and so peremptory in its terms, as to insure implicit obedience. This instrument having been drafted and approved, was distributed according to the original plan. That which was addressed to the people inhabiting the country now comprised within the limit of King's County, was as follows:

"*To the inhabitants of the District of Grand-Pré, Minas, River Canard, etc.; as well ancient, as young men and lads*:

"Whereas, his Excellency the Governor has instructed us of his late resolution, respecting the matter proposed to the inhabitants, and has ordered us to communicate the same in person, his Excellency, being desirous that each of them should be fully satisfied of his Majesty's intentions, which he has also ordered us to communicate to you, such as they have been given to him: We therefore order and strictly enjoin, by these presents, all of the inhabitants, as well of the above-named District, as of all the other Districts, both old men and young men, as well as all the lads of ten years of age, to attend at the church at Grand-Pré, on Friday the fifth instant, at three of the clock in the afternoon, that we may impart to them what we are ordered to communicate to them; declaring that no excuse will be admitted on any pretence whatever, on pain of forfeiting goods and chattels, in default of real estate.—Given at Grand-Pré, second September, 1755, and twenty-ninth year of his Majesty's reign.

John Winslow.'

"In obedience to this summons, four hundred and eighteen able-bodied men assembled. These being shut into the church (for that too had become an arsenal), Colonel Winslow placed himself with his officers, in the centre, and addressed them thus:

"Gentlemen: I have received from his Excellency, Governor Lawrence, the King's commission, which I have in my hand; and by his orders you are convened together, to manifest to you his Majesty's final resolution to the French inhabitants of this his province of Nova Scotia; who, for almost half a century, have had more indulgence granted them than any of his subjects in any part of his dominions; what use you have made of it you yourselves best know. The part of duty I am now upon, though necessary, is very disagreeable to my natural make and temper, as I know it must be grievous to you, who are of the same species; but it is not my business to animadvert, but to obey such orders as I receive, and therefore, without hesitation, shall deliver you his Majesty's orders and instructions, namely, that your lands and tenements, cattle of all kinds and live stock of all sorts, are forfeited to the Crown; with all other your effects, saving your money and household goods, and you yourselves to be removed from this his province.

"Thus it is peremptorily his Majesty's orders, that the whole French inhabitants of these Districts be removed; and I am, through his Majesty's goodness, directed to allow you liberty to carry off your money and household goods, as many as you can without discommoding the vessels you go in. I shall do everything in my power that all those goods be secured to you, and that you are not molested in carrying them off; also that whole families shall go in the same vessel, and make this remove, which I am sensible must give you a great deal of trouble, as easy as his Majesty's service will admit: and hope that, in whatever part of the world you may fall, you may be faithful subjects, a peaceable and happy people. I must also inform you that it is his Majesty's pleasure that you remain in security under the inspection and direction of the troops I have the honor to command.'

"The poor people, unconscious of any crime, and full of concern for having incurred his Majesty's displeasure, petitioned Colonel Winslow for leave to visit their families, and entreated him to detain a part only of the prisoners as hostages; urging with tears and prayers their intention to fulfill their promise of returning after taking leave of their kindred and consoling them in their distresses and misfortunes. The answer of Colonel Winslow to this petition was to grant leave of absence to twenty only, for a single day. This sentence they bore with fortitude and resignation, but when the hour of embarkation arrived, in which they were to part with their friends and relatives without a hope of ever seeing them again, and to be dispersed among strangers, whose language, customs, and religion, were opposed to their own, the weakness of human nature prevailed, and they were overpowered with the sense of their miseries. The young men were first ordered to go on board of one of the vessels. This they instantly and peremptorily refused to do, declaring that they would not leave their parents; but expressed a willingness to comply with the order, provided they were permitted to embark with their families. The request was rejected, and the troops were ordered to fix bayonets and advance toward the prisoners, a motion which had the effect of producing obedience on the part of the young men, who forthwith commenced their march. The road from the chapel to the shore—just one mile in length—was crowded with women and children; who, on their knees, greeted them as they passed, with their tears and their blessings; while the prisoners advanced with slow and reluctant steps, weeping, praying, and singing hymns. This detachment was followed by the seniors, who passed through the same scene of sorrow and distress. In this manner was the whole male part of the population of the District of Minas put on board the five transports stationed in the river Gasperau."

Now, my dear lady; you who have followed the fortunes of Evangeline, in Longfellow's beautiful poem, and haply wept over her weary pilgrimage, pray give a thought to the rest of the 18,000 sent into a similar exile! And you, my dear friend, who have listened to the oracles of Plymouth pulpits, take a Sabbath afternoon, and calmly consider how far you may venture to place your faith upon it, whether you can subscribe to the idolatrous worship of that boulder stone, and say—

"Rock of ages cleft for me, Let me to thy bosom flee;"

or whether you measure any other act between this present time and the past eighteen hundred years, except by the eternal principles of Righteousness and Truth?

Gentle reader, as we sit in this little inn-room, and see the ragged edge of the moon shimmering over the meadows of Grand-Pré, do we not feel a touch of the sin that soiled her garments a hundred years ago? Had we not better abstain from blowing our Puritan trumpets so loudly, and wreathe with crape our banners for a season? Let us rather date from more recent achievements. Let us take a fresh start in history and brag of nothing that antedates Bunker Hill. Here everybody has a hand toapplaud. But for the age that preceded it, the least said about it the better! There, out lamp! and good night! to-morrow "Home, sweet Home!" But I love this province!

APPENDIX.

Peccavi! I hope the reader will forgive me for my luckless description of the procession to lay the corner stone of the Halifax Lunatic Asylum, in Chapter I. No person can trifle or jest with the *object* of so noble a charity. But the procession itself was pretty much as I have described it; indeed, pretty much like all the civic processions I have ever witnessed in any country. The following account of the results of that good work may interest the reader:

"A visit to the Lunatic Asylum building, on the eastern side of the harbor, furnishes some notes of interest. The walk from the ferry has very pleasing features of village, farming and woodland character. The building stands on a rising ground, which commands a noble view of the western bank of the harbor opposite; northward, of the Narrows and Basin; and southward, of the islands, headlands and ocean. The medical superintendent of the institution is actively engaged carrying out plans toward the completion of the building, and gives very courteous facilities to visitors. The part of the Asylum which now appears of such respectable dimensions is just one-third part of the intended building. It is expected to accommodate ninety patients; the completed building, two hundred and fifty. The private and public rooms, cooking, serving, heating and other apartments appear to be very judiciously arranged, with an eye to good order, cheerfulness and thorough efficiency. The building is well drained, defective mason-work has been remedied, and all appears steadily advancing towards the consummation of wishes long entertained by its philanthropic projectors. The building is to be lighted with gas manufactured on the premises; all the apartments are to be heated by steam; and the water required for various purposes of the establishment, after being conveyed from the lakes, is to be raised to the loft immediately under the roof, and there held in tanks, ready for demand. The roofing we understand to be a model for lightness of material and firmness of construction. The heating apparatus occupies the underground floor. It consists of numerous coils of metal tubes, to which the steam is conveyed from an out-building, which contains the furnace and other apparatus. From the hot-air apartment the warm air is conveyed, by means of flues, to the various rooms of the building, each flue being under the immediate control of the officers of the institution. Ventilation is obtained by flues communicating with the space just below the roof; and the impure air is expected to pass off through openings in the cupola which rises above the roof ridges. By the heating apparatus the danger and trouble consequent on numerous fires are avoided, at about the same expense which the common mode would cause. Very judicious arrangements for drainage, laying off the grounds, etc., appear to have been adopted, and are in progress. The building is to be approached by a gracefully curved carriage road. The grounds are to be surrounded by a hawthorn fence, immediately within which will be a shaded, thoroughly drained path for walking. The slopes of the hill in front are in course of levelling, and will soon present a scene of lawn and grain field; while a southwest area is laid off as an extensive garden and nursery of trees and shrubs. This important appendage to such an institution is charmingly situated, as regards scenery; and, with its terraces, plantation, vegetable and flower departments, etc., will soon be a very admirable place of resort for purposes of sanitary toil, or retirement and rest. We rejoice that, altogether, the establishment promises to be a very decided proof of provincial advance, and a credit to the country. After all the difficulties, delays and doubts that have occurred, this is a very gratifying result. The building is expected to be ready for reception of patients sometime in September, or the early part of October."—*Halifax Morning Sun, June 14, 1858.*

Halifax.—The following letter of a correspondent of the *New York Times* may interest the reader. It is a very fair account of the aspect of the chief city of this Province:

"The Lieutenant-Governor, Sir J. Gaspard le Marchant, is said to be a severe disciplinarian. He served in the wars of the Peninsula, and is now being rewarded for his distinguished services as Governor of this Province. He reviews the troops twice a week upon the Common, and is very strict. The evolutions of the rank and file are the most perfect exhibitions of the kind I have ever witnessed. During one of these reviews I took occasion to remark to a citizen that they were *almost* equal to the Seventh Regiment of New York. The bystanders laughed incredulously. The bands are as perfect in movement as the troops. The whole affair passes off literally like clock-work, a pendulum being kept in sight of the reviewing officers, by which to measure the music of the bands, and step of the soldiers. Each review concludes with a presentation of the royal standard—the identical colors which were first

unfurled upon the Redan by this regiment at the fall of
Sebastopol. The ceremony is impressive, an almost superstitious
reverence being paid to the triumphant bunting. The review ended,
the band remains for a half hour to play for the entertainment of
the citizens, who generally attend in large numbers.

"There are among the officers and soldiers of the 62d and 63d
many bearing upon their left breasts the Victoria medal, and other
decorations bestowed for distinguished bravery at Sebastopol. The
most eminent of these is Colonel Ingall, who has both breasts
covered with these testimonials of bravery. They are not, however,
confined to the officers, but many of the rank and file are favored
in like manner.

"The military as a whole are popular among the citizens, and
many of the officers, and not a few of the privates since their
return from the Crimea, have stormed other Malakoffs, when the
victory has been as signal, if the risks have not been as great,
carrying off, as trophies, some of the finest girls in the place.

"Upon entering this harbor from the sea the principal objects of
interest to a stranger are the fortifications which line its two sides,
the first three or four being round castles pierced for two tiers of
guns, and having temporary wooden roofs thrown over them to
protect the works; they are situated upon prominent points and
islands commanding both entrances. The first principal fort is
that situated at the junction of the 'northwest arm' with the harbor.
This is a granite structure of some pretensions, and during the
past season was, with the high, level lands which surround it,
made the head-quarters or camping-ground for the troops. Tents

here covered all the hill-side, presenting a very picturesque appearance; camp life was adopted in all its details, and the most thorough drilling was gone through with, including the digging of trenches, throwing up earth-works, etc. The fortifications upon George's Island, just below the town, are being extended and strengthened, and when completed, will be the principal defence of the harbor. The Citadel or Fort George, occupies the high, round hill which rises directly back of the town, to about three hundred feet above the tide, and perfectly commands the town and adjacent harbor. There is said to be room enough within its walls for all the inhabitants of the town, to which they could retreat in case of a siege. From a personal inspection, however, I judge they would have to pack them pretty closely. The works cover an area of about six acres, there being a double line of forts, composed of massive granite, and presenting every variety of angle. A ditch twenty-five feet deep and sixty feet wide surrounds it on all sides, with a single entrance or bridgeway, on the east aide, which could be removed in an hour. Two ravelins, which have been lately completed within the walls, are elegant specimens of masonry. The whole hill is being rounded off, and a line of earth-works are to be constructed at its base at every salient angle. The parapet is now covered at wide intervals, with 32-pounders, mounted upon iron carriages. Extensive changes and improvements are being adopted, and when the present plans are complete, this fort, it is said, will mount over 400 guns. The cast-iron swivel carriages are condemned as being too liable to injury from cannon-shots, and are all to be replaced by others made of teak-wood.

"There exists, evidently, some reluctance among the officers in command to a close inspection of these works by foreigners. An instance in point occurred to-day. There were two young men, Americans, looking at the fort. They had obtained permission, which is given in writing by the Quartermaster-General, to inspect the Signal-Station, etc., but they were observed with paper and pencil in hand, taking down particular memoranda of the fortification, the size of guns, their number, the positions of the ravelins and what not. As this was considered a palpable breach of courtesy, a sergeant tapped them on the shoulder and led them out of the gate, with a reprimand for what he called their want of good manners. It is a long time since anything of the kind has occurred.

"This Citadel is the place from which all vessels are signalled to the town. The signal stations are four in number; the first being at the Citadel, the second at 'York Redcut,' five miles down the harbor, the third, 'Camperdown,' some ten miles further, and the fourth, with which this last signals, is the island of 'Sambro,' ten miles south of the entrance to the harbor. The system is carried on by means of a series of black balls, which are hoisted in different positions upon two yard-arms, a long and a short one, placed one above the other on a tall flag-staff. The communication is very rapid, and is exempt from liability to mistakes. A sentence transmitting an order of any kind from one of the lower stations is sent and received in less than two minutes. The distance from 'Sambro,' the outer station, is about twenty miles from the Citadel. Maryatt's code of marine signals is in use here. The new marine code, lately issued under the auspices of the London Board

---

of Trade, 'for all nations,' is pronounced by the operator as too complicated to become of any practical use, necessitating, as it would, the employment of a 'flag-lieutenant' on board every ship, who should do nothing but the signalling, since not one captain in a hundred would ever have the time or patience to acquaint himself with its mysteries.

"Some works of internal improvement are in progress, which will be important in promoting the prosperity and in developing the resources of this Province. A railroad across the Isthmus to Truro, with a branch-road to Windsor, will connect the interior towns with Halifax, and furnish modern facilities for communication with the other Provinces and with the States. Twenty-two miles of the road are already completed, and the remainder will be finished soon. A canal is also in progress from the head of Halifax harbor (north side) in the direction of Truro, which is to connect a remarkable chain of lakes with the Shubenacadie River, which empties into Minas' Basin at the head of the Bay of Fundy. Great results are anticipated in favor of the farming and other interests along its route. The work is in an advanced stage towards completion.

"There is, it is said, no portion of the American Continent so abundantly supplied with water communication as Nova Scotia. The whole interior is a continuous chain of lakes. The coast is rocky and most unpromising, but the interior is said to contain some of the best farming land east of Illinois. Hon. Albert Pillsbury, the American Consul, who is thoroughly conversant with the resources of the Province, declares it, in his opinion, the richest portion of the American Continent—richest in coal, minerals and agricultural resources. Mr. Pillsbury takes advantage of his well-deserved popularity in the Province to tell the Blue Noses some home truths. On one occasion he told them it was evident the Lord knew they were the laziest people on the earth, and had, therefore, taken pity on them, and given them more facilities for transacting their business than were possessed by any other people under the sun.

"In the newspaper line Nova Scotia appears to be fully up to the spirit of the age. The following is a list of all kinds published in the Province:

"*Tri-Weeklies.*—Morning Journal, Morning Chronicle, Morning Advertiser, the Sun, and British Colonist.

"*Weeklies.*—Acadian Recorder, Nova Scotian, Weekly Sun, and Weekly Colonist.

"*Religious (?).*—Church Times, Episcopal; Presbyterian Witness, Presbyterian Church of Nova Scotia, etc.; Monthly Record, Established Church of Scotland or Kirk; Christian Messenger, Baptist; Catholic, Roman Catholic; Wesleyan, Methodist.

"*Temperance.*—The Abstainer.

"*Weeklies.*—Yarmouth Herald, published at Yarmouth; Yarmouth Tribune (semi-weekly); Liverpool Transcript, Liverpool; Western News, Bridgetown; Avon Herald (semi-weekly), Windsor; Eastern Chronicle, Pictou; Antigonish Casket, Antigonish; Cape Breton News, Sidney, C. B.

"In telegraphs they are better supplied than any other portion of the world of equal territory, and the same number of inhabitants. There are thirty-nine offices, and 1,300 miles of telegraphic wire in this Province.

"The Reciprocity Treaty has largely increased the trade of Nova Scotia, but the means of intercommunication are still far behind the wants of the people. When it was proposed a year ago to place a steamer upon the line from Halifax to Boston, to carry freight and passengers, the idea was scouted as chimerical, and certain to fail. The Eastern State, a Philadelphia-built propeller of 330 tons, was purchased and commenced to ply fortnightly; she has accommodations for fifty passengers, and two hundred tons of freight. She has seldom had less than fifty passengers upon any trip, and upon the last one from Halifax there were one hundred and sixty-three. The fare from Boston to Halifax is $10, meals included. She has also had a good supply of freight, and has cleared for her owners the last year over $2,500. Captain Killam, her commander, is highly esteemed, for his sailorly and gentlemanly qualities. In the opinion of shrewd business men, a steamer would pay between this and New York direct. At present, Boston virtually controls the fish-market in part by her intimate relations with the Provinces, and New York buys second-hand from them, when they might as well have their fish from first hands.

"Government lands are to be purchased in any quantity at $1 per acre, and by an act of the Provincial Legislature, aliens are as free to purchase as native citizens or residents. Several American capitalists have availed themselves of the opening, and invested largely in the 'timber and farming lands of Nova Scotia, and an infusion of this element is all that is required to develop a prosperous future for this Province.'

"Saile."

"Tories.—The number of loyalists who arrived in Nova Scotia was very great. They constituted a large proportion of the original settlers in almost every section of the colony. So termed because of their loyalty to the sovereign, and unwillingness to remain in the revolted and independent States, they found their way hither chiefly in the years 1783-4. Sometimes termed refugees, because of their seeking refuge on British soil from those with whom they had contended in the great Revolutionary struggle, the names are often interchanged, whilst sometimes they are joined together in the title of 'Loyalist Refugees.' No less than 20,000 arrived prior to the close of the year in which the Independence of the United States was acknowledged. These chose spots suited to their inclinations, if not always adapted to their wants, in the counties of Digby, Annapolis, Guysboro', Shelburne, and Hants. In these five counties, for the most part, are resident the children of the loyalists, though, as hinted, they are to be met with in smaller companies elsewhere.

"We cannot doubt that the purest motives and highest sense of duty actuated very many, though not all, of this vast number, when they turned their backs upon the houses and farms, the pursuits and business, the friends and relations of past years. To this may, in some measure, be attributed the marked loyalty of this province. Principles of obedience to the laws, and allegiance to the crown, were instilled into the minds of their children, who in their turn handed down the sentiments of their ancestors until the good leaven spread, and tended to strengthen that loyalty which already existed in the hearts of the people. More than once has this trait been manifested by our countrymen in town and country. When the first blood of the rebellion in Canada was shed in 1837, meetings were held in every village and settlement in the province, each proclaiming in fervent language the deepest attachment to the sovereign and the government, while in Halifax the people determined to support the wives and children of the absent troops. When two years later the inhabitants of the State of Maine prepared to invade New Brunswick, the announcement was received with intense feelings of regard for the honor of the British Crown. The House, which was then sitting, voted £100,000, and 8,000 men to aid the New Brunswickers in repelling the invaders, and rising in a body gave three cheers for the queen, and three for their loyal brethren of the sister province. Long may the feeling continue to exist, and grow within our borders! long may we remain beneath the mild away of that gracious queen, whose virtues shed lustre on the crown she wears! long may every Nova Scotian's voice exclaim, 'God save our noble Queen.'"—*Nova Scotia and Nova Scotians*, by Rev. Geo. W. Hill, A.M.

"Negroes.—There are to be found in the colony some five thousand negroes, whose ancestors came to the province in four distinct bodies, and at different times. The first class were originally slaves, who accompanied their masters from the older colonies; but as the opinion prevailed that the courts would not recognize a state of slavery, they were liberated. On receiving their freedom they either remained in the employment of their former owners, or obtaining a small piece of land in the neighborhood, eked out a miserable existence, rarely improving their condition, bodily or mental.

"There were, secondly, a number of free negroes, who arrived at the conclusion of the American Revolutionary war; but an immense number of these were removed at their own request to Sierra Leone, being dissatisfied with both the soil and climate.

"Shortly after the removal of these people, the insurgent negroes of Jamaica were transported to Nova Scotia; they were known by the name of Maroons in the island, and still termed so, on their landing at Halifax. Their story is replete with interest: during their brief stay in Nova Scotia they gave incredible trouble from their lawless and licentious habits, in addition to costing the government no less a sum than ten thousand pounds a year. Their idleness and gross conduct at last determined the government to send them, as the others, to Sierra Leone, which was accordingly done in the year 1803, after having resided at Preston for the space of four years.

"The last arrival of Africans in a body was at the conclusion of the second American War in 1815, when a large number were permitted to take refuge on board the British squadron, blockading the Chesapeake and southern harbors, and were afterwards landed at Halifax. The blacks now resident in Nova Scotia are descendants chiefly of the first and last importations—the greater part of the two intermediate having been removed. Even some of these last were transported by their own wish to Trinidad, while those who remained settled down at Preston and Hammonds Plains, or wandered to Windsor and other places close at hand.

"But little changed in any respect—their persons and their property—they have passed through much wretchedness during the last half century. Their natural indolence and love of ease being ill suited to our latitude, in which a long and severe winter demands unceasing diligence, and more than ordinary prudence, in those who depend upon manual labor for their means of subsistence. Amongst them, however, are to be found a few who are prudent, diligent and prosperous. These are worthy of the more esteem, in proportion as they have met with greater obstacles, and happily have surmounted them."—*Ibid.*

Eminent Men.—Besides many gentlemen of rare talents, distinguished in the annals of the province, the following Nova Scotians have won a more extended reputation: Sir Edward Belcher, the famous Arctic navigator; Rear-Admiral Provo Wallis, who captured our own vessel the Chesapeake, after the death of his superior, Captain Brooke. The words of Lawrence, "Don't give up the ship," record the memorable achievement of this naval officer. Donald McKay, who after perfecting his education in New York as a ship-builder, removed to Boston, Massachusetts, and there has won for that city distinguished honors; Thomas C. Haliburton, the author of "Sam Slick," and a great number of other clever books; Samuel Cunard, the father of the Cunard line! who does not know him? General Beckwith, not less known in the annals of philanthropy; Gilbert Stuart Newton, artist; General Inglis, the defender of Lucknow, and General William Fenwick

Williams, the hero of Kars. The mere mention of such names is sufficient—their eulogy suggests itself.

Footnotes

[A] Adam Clark's "Commentary on Book of Kings." II. Samuel, chap. iii.

[B] This William Alexander, Earl of Sterling, was the ancestor of General Lord Sterling, one of the most distinguished officers in the American Revolution.

[C] The name "Acadia," is, no doubt, a primitive word, from the Abenaqui tongue—we find it repeated in *Tracadie*, *Shubenacadie*, and elsewhere in the province.

[D] One incident will suffice to show the character of these forays. A small island on Passamaquoddy Bay was invaded by the forces under Col. Church, at night. The inhabitants made no resistance. All gave up; "but," says Church in his dispatch to the governor, "looking over a little run, I saw something look black just by me: stopped and heard a talking; stepped over and saw a little hut, or wigwam, with a crowd of people round about it, which was contrary to my former directions. I asked them what they were doing? They replied, 'there were some of the enemy in a house, and would not come out.' I asked what house? They said, 'a bark house' I hastily bid them pull it down, *and knock them on the head, never asking whether they were French or Indians, they being all enemies alike to me.*" Such was the merciless character of these early expeditions to peaceful Acadia.

"Herod of Galilee's babe-butchering deedLives not on history's blushing page alone;Our skies, it seems, have seen like victims bleed,And our own Ramahs echoed groan for groan;The fiends of

France, whose cruelties decreedThose dexterous drownings in the Loire and Rhone,Were, at their worst, but copyists, second-hand,Of our shrined, sainted sires, the Plymouth Pilgrim band."

[E]In the treaty of Utrecht, no mention was made either of the Indians or of their lands.

[F]Charlevoix.

[G]Since my visit this work has actually commenced. At the close of the legislative session of 1857, the Hon. Joseph Howe moved, and the Hon. Attorney-General seconded, and the House, after some demur, resolved, that his Excellency be requested to appoint a commission for examining and arranging the records of the Province. Dining the recess the office was instituted, and Thomas B. Akins, Esq., a gentleman distinguished for antiquarian taste and research, was appointed commissioner. It was known that in the garrets or cellars of the Province Building were heaps of manuscript records, of various kinds; but their exact nature and value were only surmised. Some of these had vanished, it is said, by the agency of rats and mice; and moth and mold were doing their work on other portions. To stay the waste, to ascertain what the heaps contained, and to arrange documents at all worthy of preservation, the commission was appointed. Mr. Akins has been for some months at the superintendence of the work, helped by a very industrious assistant, Mr. James Farquhar. Very pleasing results indeed have been realized. Several boxes of documents, arranged and labelled, have been packed, and fifteen or twenty volumes of interesting manuscripts have been prepared. Some of these are of great interest, relative to the history of the Province, and of British America generally, being original papers concerning the conquest and settling of the Provinces, and having reference to the Acadian French, the Indians, the taking of Louisburgh, of Quebec, and other matters of historic importance connected with the suppression of French dominion in America. We understand some of these documents prove, as many previously believed, that what appeared to be a stern necessity, and not wanton oppression or tyranny, caused the painful dispersion of the former French inhabitants of the more poetic and pastoral parts of Acadia. If this be so, some excellent sentiment and eloquent romance will have to be taken with considerable modification. A few of the most indignant bursts (?) in Longfellow's fine poem of "Evangeline" may be in this predicament; and may have to be read, not exactly as so much gospel, but rather as rhetorical extremes, unsubstantial, but too elegant to be altogether discarded. In volumes alluded to, of the record commission, the dispatches, and letters, and other documents of a former age, and in the handwriting, or from the immediate dictation, of eminent personages, will present very attractive material for those who find deep interest in such venerable inquiries; who obtain from this kind of lore a charming renewal of the past, a clearing up of local history, and an almost face-to-face conference with persons whose names are landmarks of national annals. The commission not only examines and arranges, but forms copious characteristic "contents" of the volumes, and an index for easy reference; it also keeps a journal of each day's proceedings. The "contents" tell the nature and topics of each document, and will thus facilitate research, and prevent much injurious turning over of the manuscripts. The work, too long delayed, has been happily commenced. Its neglect was felt to be a fault and a reproach, and serious loss was known to impend; but still it was put off, and spoken lightly of, and sneered at, and a very mistaken economy pretended, until last legislative session, when it was adopted by accident apparently, and is now in successful operation. The next questions are, how will the arranged documents be preserved? who will have them in charge? will they be allowed to be scattered about in the hands of privileged persons, to be lost wholesale? or will they, as they should, be sacredly conserved, a store to which all shall have a common but well-guarded light of access and research.— *Halifax Sun, Dec. 9, 1857.*

[H]Poem by the Hon. Joseph Howe.

[I]At the present moment, the poor in the Township of Clare are maintained by the inhabitants at large; and being members of one great family, spend the remainder of their days in visits from house to house. An illegitimate child is almost unknown in the settlements.

The End